Hunger

THE ART OF LIVING SERIES
Series Editor: Mark Vernon

From Plato to Bertrand Russell philosophers have engaged wide audiences on matters of life and death. *The Art of Living* series aims to open up philosophy's riches to a wider public once again. Taking its lead from the concerns of the ancient Greek philosophers, the series asks the question "How should we live?". Authors draw on their own personal reflections to write philosophy that seeks to enrich, stimulate and challenge the reader's thoughts about their own life. In a world where people are searching for new insights and sources of meaning, *The Art of Living* series showcases the value of philosophy and reveals it as a great untapped resource for our age.

Published
Clothes   *John Harvey*
Deception   *Ziyad Marar*
Fame   *Mark Rowlands*
Hunger   *Raymond Tallis*
Illness   *Havi Carel*
Pets   *Erica Fudge*
Sport   *Colin McGinn*
Wellbeing   *Mark Vernon*
Work   *Lars Svendsen*

Forthcoming
Death   *Todd May*
Middle Age   *Chris Hamilton*
Sex   *Seiriol Morgan*

Hunger

Raymond Tallis

ACUMEN

First published in 2008 by Acumen

Acumen Publishing Limited
Stocksfield Hall
Stocksfield
NE43 7TN
www.acumenpublishing.co.uk

ISBN: 978-1-84465-155-9

British Library Cataloguing-in-Publication Data
A catalogue record for this book is available
from the British Library.

Designed and typeset by Kate Williams, Swansea.
Printed and bound by Biddles Ltd, King's Lynn.

Contents

Acknowledgements

I am very grateful to Mark Vernon and Steven Gerrard, without whom this book would not have come into being, and for their enthusiasm and support during its composition. I am also grateful to Kate Williams for her scrupulous and careful copy-editing.

Hors d'oeuvre: human is hungry

The complex history of humanity and of our individual lives is most essentially the history of our hungers, and our endeavours to satisfy them. Our accidental and accident-prone lives begin not with a cry of joy, or of surprise at our existence, but of need. From our first breath to our last we are enclosed in a fundamental existential truth: that there is a gap between the state we are in and the state we would like to be in. Hunger is the experience of that gap, from which arises our misery and our joy, our hope and our despair, our wretchedness and our glory.

Any investigation of hunger conducted at the appropriate depth will quickly widen into an enquiry into human nature and the relationship between humanity and nature. It will soon be overwhelmed by the seemingly limitless variety of the pangs felt by the human animal. The nature of hunger – its objects and its subjective content – varies dramatically through our lives. The voracious infant raging at the empty breast will grow up into a person hungry for pleasure, success, self-esteem, power, possessions, or even for a life that seems to have a deeper or more coherent meaning. To be human is to be hungry, yes, but it is also to change hunger from a given by which we are defined to needs, passions, desires, by which we define ourselves.

Many, in some cases most, of the hungers that occupy our lives are not seen in the natural world. Even the "given" hunger – biological hunger – is transformed. At the very basic level, the fact that, as Marx and Engels pointed out, we produce the means

1

of our subsistence, places eating at a great distance from animal feeding; and when we starve, the causes are as likely to be political as natural, to have their origins within the actions of our fellow men rather than in the processes of nature. If I were to identify the most important message of this book it would be this: notwithstanding the chastening effects of biological hunger, we humans are not to be understood in biological terms.

To this extent *Hunger* is a small act of resistance against the increasingly strong tide of opinion that human beings are at bottom "just animals" and they are "at top" what they are at bottom. A convergence of evolutionary theory, neuroscience and other biological disciplines has led countless thinkers to claim that we are best understood as organisms whose entire panoply of behaviour is directly or indirectly related to organic survival. The human being, we are told, is a phenotype just as in thrall to the survival of the selfish genome as an ape, a frog or a cockroach. If we are distinguished from other members of the animal kingdom, it is only a matter of our greater complexity; and, more specifically, of our ability to deceive ourselves into thinking that we have free will and that we act for reasons other than individual or group self-interest dictated by instincts.

Unfortunately, this biologism seems to have common sense and honesty on its side. The shallow knowingness that sees human hungers as essentially unreformed animal instincts – as being, or boiling down to, physiological hunger – is, however, wrong for a variety of reasons.

First, it overlooks the extraordinary achievements of humanity. The meanest artefact, the least complex communication, the most trivial everyday decision, the most commonplace of thoughts, goes way beyond anything seen in the animal kingdom, tapping into an almost boundless nexus of ideas, concepts, shared memories and layers of self-consciousness. One does not have to invoke symphonies, cities and the great monuments of knowledge, such as biomedical science itself, to encounter the yawning gulf between ourselves and beasts. A reflection on how, when and with what accompanying feelings we greet or withhold a greeting from someone with whom we sit down to eat is sufficient.

Secondly, biologism undermines hope for a better future. The link between animalist accounts of humanity and nihilistic despair has been increasingly clear over the past two centuries. Its most prominent recent manifestation is in some strains of Green thinking, where human beings are regarded as vermin that have over-run the planet and deserve the fate of other vermin before them. This link is most clearly exemplified in the hugely popular writings of the philosopher John Gray, for whom planet earth has been doomed by the arrogance of human beings (*"Homo rapiens"*) who fail to acknowledge their status as animals, believe that they have access to scientific truth and fantasize that they can alter things for the better. This attitude of contempt for the intellectual, technical and political achievements of mankind is, if it is taken seriously, dangerous as well as wrong. Gray's assertion that man is just an animal (and a rather nasty one at that) leads him to the conclusion that *"Homo rapiens* is only one of very many species and not obviously worth preserving" (Gray 2002: 151). It may be alarmist to suggest that Gray's ideas are anything other than the idle musings of a misanthrope, but it is important to remember that when human beings in particular regard human beings in general as animals, they may be inclined to treat one another even worse than hitherto in the domestic, local political and geopolitical spheres. One consequence of this is that those who are hungry are more likely to remain so.

Thirdly, misunderstanding the nature of human hunger, and your own hungers, is a serious impediment to trying to make the most of your life. The art of living consists in great part in managing your hungers so that they do not destroy your own or anyone else's happiness. Satisfying them, coming to terms with them, controlling them, escaping from them, or even putting them to good use – perhaps in dealing with others' more basic hungers, helping to liberate the undernourished so that they, too can experience the higher hungers – these are the challenges to a life well lived. It is therefore of the greatest importance that we are able to understand our hungers; or at least to see them for what they are; or, at the very least, not see them for what they are not.

More broadly, we need to understand ourselves in a way that, while it takes account of our biological roots, acknowledges that we have moved far beyond those roots. This journey was prefigured in the mystery that is evident even in biological hunger: *the fact that it is experienced at all.* At any rate, hunger is a good way of exploring the complex relationship between the biological and non-biological in us; in short, of seeing more clearly the extraordinary creatures we are. In this respect, I have a precursor in Leon Kass whose magnificent book *The Hungry Soul* – perceptive, rich, wise and humane – I came across only when this present book was well under way. Kass (to use his own words) "treats certain common phenomena of eating ... primarily as evidence in [the] search for what is universally, permanently, and profoundly true about the human animal and its deepest hungerings" (1999: xi). Although he and I cover very different territory and cite a different literature, my enquiries are conducted very much in the spirit of his philosophical anthropology.

If I seem to be protesting a little too vigorously about the value of philosophizing about hunger, it is because I fear that some readers may find something distasteful about choosing to reflect on hunger, except with the aim of alleviating its most literal and basic forms. For many, basic biological hunger is not merely an interesting theme of philosophical enquiry but unremitting hell on earth.

According to the World Health Organization, 800 million people in developing countries suffer from chronic hunger: it is the world's major health risk. Even in the USA, the richest nation in history, one in ten citizens live in "food-insecure" households, starving amid other people's plenty. In developing countries the combination of poverty, war, civil unrest and bad (wicked, corrupt, idle, indifferent) governance means that millions of children go to bed each night in an agony of malnutrition and many do not survive to adult life. In the face of such facts, philosophizing about hunger may seem ethically dubious. Most human beings who have ever lived have simply suffered hunger and acted as best as they could to limit their suffering.

It seems to me likely that the deepest differences between human beings are not between man and woman, black and white, between intellectuals who aspire to the examined life and the thoughtless who do not, between those who do and those who do not believe in God, but between the hungry and the well-fed. For the hungry, philosophical reflections on the nature and transformations of hunger count for very little, less perhaps than the minute comfort of sucking a pebble. Eating "the acorns and grass of knowledge ... for the sake of truth" – Nietzsche's description of true philosophy – would seem a somewhat luxurious hardship to those eating acorns and grass to quiet the savage and unending pangs of hunger. Hunger and its effects seem like a critique of philosophy and of the value placed on "the examined life". I feel pretty confident that a few days without food would be sufficient to put paid to my interest in the metamorphoses of hunger examined in the chapters that follow.

There is nothing uniquely reprehensible in philosophizing about hunger. It is certainly no worse than engaging in many other diversions in the full knowledge that one is not lifting a finger to alleviate suffering of one's malnourished fellow human beings. The millions of person centuries that are devoted to discussing the fortunes of a particular football club or sporting star or the career of a rising opera singer are just as hardhearted. I want, however, to defend philosophizing about hunger on stronger grounds than that it is no worse than recreational prattling.

Making human hunger less obvious than it seems and following its metamorphoses in those who live above subsistence level seems justified if it promotes the kind of reflection that could slow the bonfire of consumption that occupies us for most of our waking hours. Or if it helped us to understand why, for most of us, for the greater past of our lives, we are less concerned than we might be about those whom we see starving on our televisions and whose unbearable miseries are reported in the daily press. As I shall argue in the final chapter, we need to think more deeply about how we affluent are to live in the future in such a way as not to threaten the prospects of those who are hoping to escape from destitution. Whether or not the present philosophical enquiry into hunger justifies itself in this way is for the reader to decide.

It will soon be evident that this book is not an empirical investigation of, even less a treatise on, the biology, culture or politics of hunger, eating and food – nine vast topics – but a very general meditation on hunger, its transformation in human beings and the relationship it has to emerging ends and aims of human life. And there is not much in the way of sustained argument in what follows; rather, an attempt at descriptive philosophical anthropology. I begin, in Chapter 1, with the nature and evolution of biological hunger, consider the extent to which a biological approach captures – and fails to capture – eating in human beings, and ask what the response to starvation does or does not tell us about human nature. In Chapter 2, I look at how the incidental pleasure of meeting nutritional needs has, in human beings, spawned a multitude of other pleasures, directly, indirectly and often only symbolically, related to culinary delight, and how the pursuit of ever-proliferating pleasures, and the avoidance of the boredom that comes with satiety, become lifelong preoccupations in those who are lucky enough to pass their lives a long way above the subsistence threshold. Chapter 3 examines the distinctive nature of human consciousness as a route into understanding the difference between the hunger associated with appetites and the no less real pangs of desire, whose supreme object is another person. "The hunger for others" is examined partly through the lens of the Hegelian insight that humans, being self-conscious, can be satisfied only by another self-consciousness, and partly through the lens of ideas that I have developed elsewhere about the distinctive nature of human consciousness. Chapter 4 deals with various manifestations of what I call the "fourth hunger": a hunger for meaning and significance that goes beyond the cycles of appetite and satiety, desire and its extinction or dissatisfaction, and that engages with the fear and sense of emptiness that assails the "knowing animal". The final chapter, which is concerned ultimately with the hunger of others, asks how we might manage our individual and collective hungers better so that we shall be less possessed by them and more concerned with the suffering of those to whom even subsistence is denied.

I acknowledge that the division of the topic into these compartments is more than a little artificial but hope that the reader will understand why it was necessary. A book is always an accident of chapters; it is just that in some cases it is easier to conceal this than in others. How one deals with the potentially limitless topic of human hunger is clearly personal in other respects. Nietzsche famously emphasized the autobiographical nature of philosophy. This is not entirely fair: *all* creative writing is to some extent autobiographical, and philosophy is in most cases the least so. Nevertheless, he put us on our guard. Philosophers write about what interests them for reasons other than a pure appetite for the most general truths; and their "take" on their chosen topics will be in thrall to undeclared influences of which they themselves may be only partly aware. Philosophical questions, simply in virtue of being all-encompassing, inescapably encroach on the questioner. While we may imagine a dispassionate outside from which they may be approached, there is no such outside. This is most evidently true when it is the hungers that drive, inspire, elevate, destroy, humiliate and glorify humanity that are in question. I therefore ask forbearance of the reader, who will bring his or her own hungers to the reading of this book.

1. The first hunger

From dynamic equilibrium to dinner

The universe is restless. Every object in it is more or less transient. Towards one extreme, we have rocks, which outlast the longest gaze; towards the other, smoke, which vanishes before our eyes. Between rock and smoke are living creatures. They are born, grow, pass their lives and die over a span that is impressive by the standards of smoke, unimpressive compared with rocks.

Rocks endure because they have built-in stability; smoke does not, for the opposite reason. Why some things are stable and others are ephemeral is not fully understood. Our knowledge of what is happening at the most fundamental level is currently in great difficulties, with the two most comprehensive, powerful and majestic theories of the physical world – the general theory of relativity and quantum mechanics – at odds with one another. At the intermediate level, however, things seem a little clearer. The most comprehensive account of the patterns of evanescence and endurance is the second law of thermodynamics, the supreme, perhaps the most metaphysical, of all the laws of nature. One formulation of this law is that the sum total of things tends towards thermodynamic equilibrium in which differences – say, of temperature, or density – are ironed out. This universal tendency towards disorder or increasing "entropy" has a simple statistical explanation: there are many more ways of being disordered than being ordered and so random change will tend towards disorder.

For our present purposes, we may translate the second law of thermodynamics as follows: highly differentiated, that is to say highly ordered, structures such as living creatures are less probable than undifferentiated ones, which have a low level of order. This translation is not without its problems: a non-anthropocentric conception of "order", for example, is not easily won from the mathematics behind the second law. Nor is it clear why, if there *is* a tendency towards disorder, the universe began in a relatively undisordered state. It will, however, do, because it helps us to get a handle on our theme. At the root of hunger is the fact that living organisms are very highly ordered systems and are, consequently, improbable. They have what the physicist and prophet of molecular biology Erwin Schrödinger (1992) called "negative entropy". They are intrinsically unstable. Their endurance, unlike that of a rock, consequently has to be *earned*: their order has to be actively maintained.

The maintenance of the order seen in living matter costs energy. A living organism may, at one level, be seen as a device for securing energy exchanges with the nearest parts of the rest of the universe, on terms favourable to itself. (The relationship between order and energy is a little complex and some would regard organisms as devices for extracting "information" rather than energy from their surrounds. The ubiquitous use of the word "information", however, is a fashion that will pass.) The energy thus extracted is then used to extend, maintain and repair the organism and support its means of reproduction: above all, maintaining relative stability by correcting changes. "Life" as the great biochemist Sir Frederick Gowland Hopkins said, "is the expression of a particular dynamic equilibrium which obtains in a polyphasic system".

Spinoza's assertions in his *Ethics* that "Everything, in so far as it is in itself, endeavours to persist in its own being" (3, prop. VI) and "The endeavour wherewith a thing endeavours to persist in its being is nothing else than the actual essence of that thing" (3, prop. VII) is most clearly applicable to living creatures. A living organism is an entity whose ultimate purpose is to maintain itself – its life consists of staying alive – or, through replication, ensure the existence of things like itself. In short, it has no more intrinsic purpose than a rock: a melancholy thought, given that a rock does not apparently have to stir itself to secure continuance. This existential tautology, whereby the end of life is primarily not to end, will come to haunt mankind, but we have a long way to go before such haunting is possible.

It is fascinating to think of the dramatic metamorphoses in the means by which organisms extract their wherewithal from their surrounds. Single cell organisms pass their lives in the bath of nutrient in which they are born. While their requirements are complex (their diet includes carbon, nitrogen, sulphur, phosphorus, numerous inorganic salts and a large number of egregious micronutrients such as zinc and molybdenum), they are not able to stir themselves much to obtain them. At best they can manage a modest amount of chemotaxis: they adjust their location by swimming in directions marked out by rising gradients of goodies such as sugar or away from toxins. As organisms get more complex, nutrition becomes more sophisticated than mere foodbathing: increasingly elaborate systems devoted to obtaining, absorbing and distributing food are differentiated; and the business of obtaining food becomes more explicit and, indeed, active. These two developments do not necessarily take place in parallel.

While some highly differentiated organisms such as trees have separate systems clearly devoted to accessing nutrition (roots and leaves) and to distributing it (through the xylem and phloem), they hardly exert themselves in order to get what they need. Although the life of the plants is, according to the poet W. H. Auden, "one continuous, solitary meal", feeding is entirely passive. A little untaxing heliotropism and a tendency to grow towards water is all the effort most plants seem to expend. In the animal kingdom, the elaboration of feeding structures is paralleled by ever more complex feeding behaviours.

One is surprised sometimes that the game is worth the candle. A lot of energy goes into the growth and maintenance of organs and systems that support feeding, ingestion and digestion. In the case of higher organisms, resources are also deployed to creating and regulating the so-called internal environment – exemplified in fluid such as blood and lymph – whose temperature, pressure and chemical composition are minutely controlled, and which buffer the cells from the fluctuations of the external environment so that those cells can get on with their business relatively undisturbed. This, too, is not without considerable metabolic cost. Indeed, when one thinks of the amount of energy that all of this takes, the picture that emerges is rather reminiscent of a taxi-driver who earns only a little more from fares than he expends cruising for customers, paying for his licence and buying and servicing his cab.

The evolution of feeding behaviour as we progress through multicellular organisms towards the primates is rather astonishing. Let us look at some randomly chosen milestones. Consider, first, a couple of invertebrates. The earthworm feeds on fragments of leaves and other plant matter in the soil that it drags down into its burrow. In its own way, it is a gatherer, although it cannot see or hear. The mouth cavity opens directly into the digestive tract without any intermediate structures. In the case of the ant, things are a little more complicated. It has two sets of jaws: one for carrying the food and the other for chewing it. This clear separation of the obtaining of food from its ingestion is an anatomical key to the ability to feed other ants and hence the basis of a quasi-social life. If we move to the vertebrates, we see not only an elaboration of the anatomical struc-tures deployed in obtaining, ingesting and digesting food, but also a great extension of the physical range over which food is sought. The most remarkable expressions of this are seasonal or climate-driven migrations. With the extension of range, the sphere of awareness also widens: the bubble of the *umwelt* or experienced universe expands. Its boundaries are marked by the increasing distances at which cues to the presence of food (or water) can be detected by ever more acute telereceptors such as smell, sight and hearing. In the case of hunters, the acquisition of nutriment acquires new dimensions. The food itself has ideas of its own, most importantly not to be food. This requires more complex strategies on the part of the hunter and, possibly, working in cooperative groups or mere packs that win through weight of numbers.

We have moved a long way from bacteria bathed in their means of subsistence, exacting directly from their surroundings the where-withal to enable them to come into being and to slow their dissolution until at least they have reproduced. The journey itself makes a central puzzle of evolution visible: why is it that we have ever more complex organisms? How specific complexities arise seems pretty straightforward: the operation of natural selection on random variation over a huge period of time seems able to account for many of the things that we see. What we cannot account for – particularly if we begin with the molecular perspective that is now conventional in biology – is why the direction of travel has been towards increased complexity, to organisms that have ever higher maintenance costs. (Think again about the taxi driver.) We are familiar with the famous "arms race" whereby prey and predators get ever more cunning, with the one building progressively better defences and the other obtaining ever more powerful weapons. There is a very obvious evolutionary explanation of that, on the basis of selective survival of the better armed and the better defended. What is more difficult to explain – although evolutionary theorists do have some good models as to how it happened – is the inner competition within an evolving organism, such that increasing sophistication – differentiation into systems, improvement of the systems – brings costs that the organism itself has to deal with. Increased complexity may make the organism better equipped to cope with a wider range of environments but it brings in its wake increased improbability. Hungers become more explicit and clamant.

It has been pointed out, by Stephen Jay Gould and many others, that the seeming trend over time towards increasing complexity, climaxing by a remarkable coincidence in the organism that is judging the complexity, *Homo sapiens*, is an illusion. The vast majority of organisms today are unicellular, just as they were in Precambrian times, before the astonishing Cambrian explosion 500 million years ago that gave rise (after nearly 3 billion years of exclusively unicellular life) to the phyla to which all present day living organisms belong. "This is truly the age of the bacteria – as it was in the beginning, is now and ever shall be", as Gould says (1994: 85). Modal, or typical, levels of complexity have not changed in 500 million years and the impression that life over all has evolved to ever more complex forms, or that this is an intrinsic tendency of evolution, is due to selective noticing of more complex organisms, which will emerge as the overall range of complexity increases. Decreased complexity may be as adaptive as increased complexity.

The point of dwelling on this is to remind ourselves how *contingent* and accidental are complex creatures – notably the seemingly most complex, ourselves – and how those hungers that have such a hold on us and place our lives in the grip of practical necessity may never have come about. It is sometimes difficult to see this contingency in our necessarily *post hoc* view of our origins. And this relates to another issue: the fact that the more complex creatures are more aware. That we *experience* our hungers is more puzzling than it may appear at first sight.

Living tissue is largely unaware of the things it needs, or of their lack. Bacteria, we may reasonably suppose, do not have a distinctive ache, thirst, pang or malaise associated with a lack of molybdenum or even of oxygen. Sentience, so far as we can tell, is very much a latecomer in the evolutionary process. Needs, and the consequences of their not being met, are explicit as hungers, as unpleasant sensations that demand relief, in only a tiny minority of organisms. Many of the most successful organisms entirely lack sentience. Micro-organisms have been around for 3.5 billion years; bees and ants have not needed to evolve for 50 to 100 million years; while man arrived perhaps 2 million years ago. Indeed, the key to evolutionary success is more likely to be something as down to earth as the ability to exhibit great diversity and flexibility in metabolic strategies and low metabolic costs. Suffering your needs does not seem to be a particularly smart way of getting ahead of the competition. From the point of view of maximizing the chances of replication of the genome, it seems at least as likely that better mechanisms should have evolved as that consciousness-led behaviour did. When we think of the extraordinary things that can be achieved by means of entirely insentient processes – for example, the growth of the brain *in utero* – the benefits of consciousness seem less self-evident. And, as we have already noted, by far the greatest part of the ascent up "Mount Improbable" – Richard Dawkins's metaphor for the evolution of complex organisms – takes place without sentience of any kind. The assumption that a teeny-weeny scrap of consciousness can give one an edge over the competition and a little more consciousness gives one more of an edge, so that selective pressures may favour ever more conscious creatures, is just that: an assumption. There is no reason why the alternative path of ever more effective mechanisms should not have been the only way forward; after all, it is overwhelmingly the way things have gone.

That the biosphere is almost entirely insentient and its dominant species are remote from anything like being conscious is hardly surprising: a series of accidents leading to increasing awareness being wrung out of the unaware processes of physics seems difficult to accommodate in the physicalist world picture of contemporary biology. And, what is more, doing something deliberately – one of the manifestations of consciousness at its highest level – seems a second best to mechanisms that allow it to happen spontaneously, if only because mechanisms are, by definition, more reliable. Consciousness may as often confuse as well as illuminate. Indeed, when we conscious creatures try to learn to do something well, we do so by handing it over to mechanisms so that it seems to happen effortlessly rather than being done deliberately, as when we walk, catch a ball or play scales on the piano. At any rate, if the blind laws of physics were good enough to bring complex organisms into being, it would seem odd that something as vague and fallible as consciousness should confer advantage. Admittedly, consciousness at the highest level seems to enable one to model possibilities and try out strategies without exposing one's self to their consequences. This does not, however, seem to compensate for the loss of the reliability that is built into the unbreakable laws of nature. The suggestion made by David Hodgson (2008) that consciousness may bring advantages because it can address a particular situation in its unique wholeness does not take account of the fact that all mechanisms are interactions between unique situations whose limits and/or wholeness are not intrinsic to them. Equally unpersuasive is the argument (Nichols & Grantham 2000) that, because phenomenal consciousness – subjective experience – is complex, it must be adaptive since *all* complex features of organisms are adaptive; and, if it is adaptive, then it must have causal efficacy.

It is true that once you are guided by conscious experience, it is prudent to remain conscious: coma renders you vulnerable because automatisms cannot take over the functions of consciousness. An unconscious human being would not make for a very long-lived zombie or robot. But this does not demonstrate that consciousness was a good thing in the first place. We tend to approach this question from the wrong end: retrospectively from the standpoint of sentient creatures, rather than prospectively, where sentience is only one of a range of strategies that might increase fitness. If, as standard Darwinian thought tells us, we are the products of "the blind forces of physics" operating in the biological realm through the intermediate pathways of molecular genetics and natural selection operating on phenotypes, it is difficult to explain the pain of hunger and the pleasure that comes with it. One would expect natural selection to favour improved mechanisms, more tightly wired into the environment, rather than rely on conscious actions, directed by a very vulnerable brain.

The emergence of sentience is mysterious for another reason: it is metabolically expensive. Metabolic costs increase in proportion to organic mass but neural tissue makes particularly high demands. By the time we reach *Homo sapiens*, the brain accounts for 20 per cent of oxygen consumption. (This probably explains why highly complex nervous systems are very rare, apart from in ourselves and the anthropoid apes. Only the cetaceans [whales and dolphins], cephalopods [squids and octopus], and elephants seem to have acquired brains that are large for their size.) In short, the standard idea that consciousness is unquestionably a good idea and that it was itself inevitable, as it has evolved to allow creatures capable of flexible action to decide among alternative courses of action on the basis of past experience and projected scenarios of possible future moves, glides over the fact that deliberate choice seems a rather inefficient way of arriving at the right thing to do, compared with having a mechanism to ensure it. Indeed, many of the more complex behaviours exhibited by higher organisms seem like attempts to deal with some of the consequences of being less snugly located in their environmental niche as a result of complexity and consciousness. This is vividly illustrated by the extent to which human beings have to be taught the survival skills that simply develop in other animals: we large-brainers have the longest periods of immaturity. While the looser connection permits flexibility, and creates elbow room for freer actions, it has delivered significant benefits in human beings in what are, in evolutionary terms, only relatively recent times, when the pooling of consciousness in a community of minds has created a second world – a human world – from which individual human beings can operate on nature as if from the outside, and on more favourable terms. Prior to that, hominids looked to be rather unpromising forms of living matter, at least compared with simpler organisms.

At the risk of seeming to prolong a digression, let us dig a little deeper. Sentience presents particular difficulties to those who subscribe to the view – subscribed to by most contemporary philosophers – that the fundamental stuff of the world is insentient matter. It is triply mysterious: it is not easy to see how it should arise (nerve impulses – the passage of ions across semi-permeable membranes – in the brain explain nothing); it is not clear that sensation-prompted behaviour is superior to ever improved mechanisms; and, given that its contents – for example, sensations of brightness and warmth (so-called secondary qualities) – do not correspond to anything intrinsic in the material world, it is not clear why they should be of any use. I mention this at this stage because it should make us challenge reductive approaches to the higher hungers – for pleasure, for the love of others, and for meaning – that see them as essentially untransformed biological needs understood in terms, ultimately, of the laws of physics.

The reader should not, at this point, be alarmed. The author is not a closet creationist or a propagandist for that most unintelligent of ideas, intelligent design. The reason that I am emphasizing that consciousness fits rather uncomfortably into the no-frills physicalism that underpins the most advanced evolutionary theory, and that it is by no means self-evident that, beyond a certain point, the pains of under-nourishment and the pleasures of feasting are necessary or even adaptive, is to remove the patina of obviousness from the notion of hunger. This is a step towards challenging the habit, evident in so many thinkers, of naturalizing human behaviour and of eliding the huge gulf between human and animal feeding behaviour. The enigma of pleasure, which tells us how far mechanistic biology is from providing an entirely satisfactory explanation of hunger, opens the way to our seeing what is in front of our noses, or indeed in our mouths: hunger, and the experiences that come with its satisfaction, are subject to transformation in the human animal not amenable to a naturalistic interpretation. A naturalistic account – which in light of the way nature is currently understood would be a materialistic account – of the hedonistic hungers, and of the vicissitudes of pleasure, described in this chapter would traduce their nature. When human beings encounter their own hungers as objects of examination, reflection and knowledge, anything is possible – as we shall see.

The transformations of dinner

When one has traced the metamorphoses of feeding – from absorbing, aspirating and filtering, to reaching out, biting and chewing, and thence to hunting and gathering – the further transformations of eating may seem rather fine print stuff. But they are not. The more carefully we look, the wider the gulf between the manner in which human beings and the manner in which all other animals interact with food. At the root of all the transformations of hunger and feeding is the fact that human beings are self-conscious and that they are conscious of one another as also being conscious. This enables the collectivization of hunger: its metamorphosis from an uncommunicated state of a solitary organism into something that is acknowledged, dealt with, anticipated, exploited, by a community of minds. The manifestations of this collectivization are protean.

While animals eat whatever their instincts place in the category "edible", the satiation of human hunger is regulated by numerous conventions. Some relate to the processing of food. The culinary revolution preceded the agricultural revolution: human beings cooked food before they grew, or domesticated, it. The agricultural revolution is itself a great mystery: why about 10,000 years ago did people change from being hunter-gatherers to farmers – and almost simultaneously in many different parts of the world? It is particularly puzzling since living by agriculture is a very poor second when compared with living by hunting and gathering. Indeed, there is evidence from pathological studies of bones of the last hunter-gatherers and the first farmers that there was a decline in the overall quality of nutrition and a reduction in the average length of life. Mithen (2005) has suggested that it was due to a combination of factors. Hunter-gathers were faced with short, abrupt climatic fluctuations at the end of the last ice age. There had been many such fluctuations before, but on this occasion human beings had different mental abilities that enabled them, for the first time, to entertain the idea of domesticating plants and animals. This not only required certain cognitive structures but also consolidated them. The agricultural revolution would have a huge impact on human time sense. The relatively small interval in hunter-gatherers between seeing food and eating it and or between seeing food, hunting it down and eating it, was greatly expanded – and changed: for the sown seed or the husbanded animal was the visible *possibility* of food, and many processes and many days would intervene between possibility and realization – between the felt need and its satisfaction. What is more, the relationship between hunger and food was altered: food was grown to meet future hungers or, as with the emergence of trade, the hungers of others who might in turn, directly or indirectly, feed one's own hunger. Hunger was collectivized.

We have moved a long way away from instincts driving behaviour and even further from stimuli producing responses. This distance is elaborated in every aspect of human nutrition. According to the structural anthropologist Claude Lévi-Strauss, the contrast between fresh raw food that has been transformed by cooking and fresh raw food that has been transformed by rotting reflects a deeper contrast; it symbolizes the contrast human beings feel, and assert, and elaborate, between culture (themselves) and nature (every-thing else) – or, perhaps, between their cultural selves and their natural bodies. This looks a little more sweeping and a little less plausible than when Lévi-Strauss enchanted *tout Paris* and intel-lectuals world-wide in the 1960s. Even so, symbolism is massively elaborated within meals, which seem to have complex, grammat-ical structures, reflecting principles that dictate which dishes can go with which and the order in which dishes should be eaten. The sequence of soup, meat and two veg, and jam roll and custard is a perfectly formed English culinary sentence. We are reminded of how different things are in the animal kingdom by the family pet next to the dinner table, which will eat anything in any order: its meals are a series of mouthfuls.

And then there are the technologies – the recipes, implements, packaging – that lie behind the simplest of meals. Every meal is the meeting point of a multitude of expertises. A piled up plate brings together not only gathered and killed life but the work of count-less hands directed by so much know-how and know-that. The link between what the body needs to maintain its dynamic equilibrium and the bodily events that secure it has now lengthened to great loops that girdle half the globe. The items that end up in the stomachs around the table will have come from other counties, other countries, other continents, and have grown in other seasons. Likewise the cutlery and crockery necessary for "civilized" eating – from Sheffield, Meissen and Taiwan – that lie together on the laid table. Even if we set aside the gastronomic League of Nations that gathers on the ordinary plate, with food brought thither from the four corners of the world, we still have an extraordinary convergence of activities, rolled up even in the food that has come from relatively nearby. Think of the steps, the processes, the competencies and the specialists that have gone into the slice of bread we dip absentmindedly into our gravy: the seed merchant, the farmer (in whose person are gathered the ploughman, the tractor maintenance man, the sower, the weeder, the harvester, the salesman), the miller, the baker and the lorry diver, to name only the most prominent characters in the wide coalition of talents that have brought the bread to the table.

The collectivization of hunger is also symbolized by the attachment of meals to times of day. These times belong to everyone, unlike the sensation of hunger, which is private. For animals, eating, if it is broken up at all (and is not a continuous activity, or passivity), takes place when an appetite encounters something it wants to eat. Eating in human beings contributes centrally to structuring the day. The scarcely formatted time of toddlerhood is structured as much by "breakfast", "lunch", "tea" and so on as by the succession of night and day. It will not be many years before the toddler will be consulting a clock that will tell her not only the time, but also to eat. And we eat by the calendar as well: we are instructed by the date as to when to feast and fast. Just how far human eating is from animal feeding is illustrated by the way meals are often connected with formalized breaks in work: the time and duration of meal breaks are the result of minute and protracted negotiations. In animals, the gathering and eating of food *is* the work. Indeed, work is not a separate part of life.

The scaffolding of ritual and convention that surrounds every aspect of eating is underlined by the extent to which meals are social occasions: opportunities for people to assert their togetherness. A dinner may be a peg on which to hang a meeting, or a pretext for other purposes: gossiping, plotting, courtship, developing a friendship, passing time, giving and receiving. The occasion is a node in an almost boundless nexus, which reminds us of the spatial and temporal distances that have been crossed in order to bring about the shared meal. And those who are gathered round the table will have come to this spot – on foot, by car, by plane – by virtue of many thousands of small actions necessary to carry out that expression of sustained purpose called a journey. The exception of the breastfeeding child, where there are not even the food inches of the hand travelling to the open mouth, underlines just how much "culture" intervenes between the hunger that signals our needs and the food that satisfies them.

The meal is concluded and the bill is requested, and we are reminded of more stretches of food miles: those we have covered in order to earn the cash to pay for it. As Marx and Engels pointed out in *The German Ideology*, "Men ... begin to distinguish themselves from animals as soon as they begin to produce the means of their subsistence" (1974: 42). This is the point at which the materials that satisfy our needs take on the form of commodities, to be generated for barter or sale, and acquired by that all-purpose quasi-commodity called "money", concerning which more presently. All of those journeys to and from, and within, work, not to speak of the journeying involved in training for work: these are wrapped up in the money that passes out of our hands in payment of the bill.

It would be possible to trace the distances between human and animal feeding in many other directions. Tables, tablecloths, table settings, table manners, for example, all demonstrate how every moment of a meal is supported by a dense network of signs. And each of these signs points to other signs. Think of what lies in the hinterland of the choice of tablemats or the folding of a napkin. Or the many rituals that connect the eating of food – and what is eaten, and how and when and with whom – with religious observances, with traditions of hospitality, with the celebration and commemoration of events, people, anniversaries, with affirming membership of human groups ranging from families to nations or religious communities. Satisfying our hunger for food is itself digested into a boundless nexus of cultural meanings given and received.

Even so, it is difficult for some to shake off the notion that there is something irreducibly animal about eating. The many steps that intervene between hunger and food reaching the stomach cannot obscure the fact that we insert food into our heads and defecate at the other end, just as a worm does. Choking and vomiting underline the continuity between the animal that merely ingests and the human who dines. But this does not justify the conclusion that our need to eat betrays how narrow is the gap between humanity and animality. Dawkins, for example, while admitting that "to force a naïve Darwinian interpretation on everything we do in our everyday lives would be an error" asserts that "we can still make a simple Darwinian interpretation of things like hunger" (Pyle 1999: 71). For some this is demonstrated by what happens to us when our fundamental biological need for food is not met: then our true, beastly, essence is unmasked.

Starvation and humanity

He smiled contemptuously at mental speculation for he remembered seeing philosophers fighting over garbage in the camp.   (Czeslaw Milosz, *The Captive Mind*)

… these are counsellors
That feelingly persuade me what I am.
                    (Shakespeare, *As You Like It*, II.i)

The first who died of hunger were men. Then children. Then women. But before the people died they frequently went insane and stopped being human beings.
                    (Ivan Stadnyuk, *People are not Angels*)

The author, and most of the readers of this book, will be part of that negligible minority in the history of humankind for whom a ready supply of good, uncontaminated food is taken for granted. It is a long time since I was truly hungry. Eating in affluent societies is, as we have discussed, dictated by custom and routine rather than hunger; it is the clock, rather than my stomach, that tells me when to eat.

While maintaining this privileged situation is a fundamental duty of government, there is no reason why it should last. The world has a nasty habit of turning one's life upside down. Nobody in Sarajevo in 1990 expected to be living on a diets of rats and scraps a few years later; and very few in Zimbabwe anticipated the policies by which the Mugabe regime has left most Zimbabweans hungry and very many actually starving, in many cases to a desperately premature death.

Astonishingly, despite its centrality in human experience, the physiology of hunger still remains unclear. We know that signals from the gut (in particular the stomach) reporting that that hollow structure is empty are sent to the hypothalamus at the base of the brain. There are probably biochemical signals related to glucose, insulin, or possibly fatty acid levels in the blood – nobody can agree – also sent to the hypothalamus. It is there that the signals to start eating (from the lateral hypothalamus) or to stop eating (from the ventromedial hypothalamus) arise.

The primary sensation of hunger is usually located in the epigastrium, where active pain is felt, as if the empty stomach seems to grow teeth and were gnawing at emptiness, like a dog trying get at the marrow in a bone picked clean. The experience of hunger is not focal, of course. The English "I am hungry" is closer to the reality than the French *J'ai faim*: hunger involves the entire body and the Sarin of privation soon permeates every aspect of the self and the world. Weakness, faintness, lassitude, apathy, irritability, light-headedness, dizziness, depression and despair are the lot of the chronically hungry. The instinct for energy conservation overrides every other impulse apart from chasing after the slightest hint of food; and the category of "food" widens. Everything becomes food. In the mass starvation caused by the Japanese war against China, "people hunted ants, devoured tree roots, ate mud" (Hastings 2007). The famished beggars who populated early modern Europe would eat dung for the seeds left in them, as did those starving in China half a millennium later in the 1930s.

In *Hunger*, his debut novel, a scream of rage for the hungry of the earth, Knut Hamsun has his hero describe the moment-to-moment experience of starvation: "My hunger was now tormenting me excruciatingly, and gave me no rest. Again and again, I swallowed saliva; I fancied it helped". Little snacks of the fluid in his own mouth are all he has to fend off the pangs. Medieval beggars would drink their own urine and plug the anus to keep the bowels feeling full. Under such circumstances, time coagulates to duration and life is pruned to mere existence: thoughts at once delirious and stale; endless hours; emptiness transformed into daggers stabbing at random. Hunger eats away at the self, at the soul. "No fear can stand up to hunger", Conrad observes in *Heart of Darkness*:

> no patience can wear it out, disgust simply does not exist where hunger is; and as to superstition, beliefs and what you may call principles, they are less than chaff in a breeze. Don't you know the devilry of lingering starvation, its exasperating torment, its black thoughts, its sombre and brooding ferocity? Well I do. It takes a man all his inborn strength to fight hunger properly. It's really easier to face bereavement, dishonesty, and the perdition of one's soul – than this kind of prolonged hunger.

The starving body begins to eat itself, like a business capitalizing its assets when revenues fail. Muscles shrink, fat disappears and – a harbinger of the skeleton-to-be – the bones protrude. There comes a point where the structures and processes that are responsible for maintaining the viability of the body begin to fail. The skin becomes thin and dry and loses its elasticity; the production of luxury tissues such as hair fails; wounds heal more slowly if at all so that a minor abrasion may turn into a chronic ulcer. The means by which the constancy of the internal environment is maintained – the condition as Claude Bernard says of free life – start to give up. The heart enlarges and then fails. The blood pressure falls. Respiration becomes slower and shallower. The energy-expensive maintenance of bodily temperature fails. The blood thins. The ability to resist infection is lost and the starveling is overwhelmed with infections, which may lead to diarrhoea and the lost of precious fluid and protein and, ironically, loss of appetite. Organ after organ and, finally, life itself fail.

How human beings behave under conditions of starvation may or may not say something about what we are. The most careful observations have been under the controlled conditions of experiment. The most drastic experiments have been unspeakable criminal activities and – with the exception of the heroic records made by Jewish doctors in the Warsaw ghetto – have not been adequately documented to provide us with useable knowledge. We do, however, have the famous Minnesota study (described in Russell 2006) carried out in the late 1940s by Ancel Keys on thirty-six volunteers, conscientious objectors, who were placed on a 1,500 calorie diet (roughly half the normal daily requirement) for six months. They lost nearly a quarter of their body weight. They knew that there was a predetermined end to their ordeal: there was warmth beyond the bleak snowfield of their privation. Their situation therefore was quite unlike that of the hundreds of millions of individuals currently alive who suffer from chronic hunger and have no good reason for expecting things to change. Nevertheless, the Minnesota volunteers underwent a rapid deterioration of personality: cheerful men became morose, flat, then bellicose, angry and chronically miserable.

Much hunger is political in origin. There is the self-inflicted starvation of the hunger-striker, who aims to speak to the conscience of his captors or to underline the rightness of his cause through a dramatic assertion of the totality of his commitment to it. The utter loss of morale and abject misery of the volunteers in Keys's experiment reminds us of the courage and iron determination of the hunger-striker (irrespective of what one thinks of his cause). Self-starvation as often brings out brutality in the captors as it speaks to their conscience. The striker literally puts his body and his life on the line, in a supreme expression of (to borrow Václav Havel's phrase) "the power of the powerless". The rituals of forced feeding using naso-gastric tubes driven down sore and bleeding orifices are particularly disgusting.

Much more commonly, political hunger is inflicted rather than chosen. Incompetence, neglect, idleness and a little malice ensured that perhaps three million people died in the Bengal famine of 1943–44, mostly by lowered resistance to disease, at a time when the *per capita* available food supply was 10 per cent higher than in 1941, a non-famine year. Ideology, and ideologically backed arrogance, which combined ill-will towards most of those outside the Communist Party with a ruthless determination to remain in power, and the appalling, boundless incompetence of a policy driven by buzzwords, lay behind the famine that Mao brought about in the Great Leap Forward of the early 1960s. Tens of millions died from starvation. Political malice is also a key element in the current famine in Zimbabwe, where at least one senior minister of the Mugabe regime, Didymus Mutasa, has expressed the view that his country would be better without those who oppose them and has directed food supplies accordingly.

One of the most catastrophic examples of malice-and-ideology-driven political starvation was the *Holdomor* or "murder by starvation" in the Ukraine in 1932–33, when about four million people, nearly 20 per cent of the Ukrainian population, died. Stalin was determined to extinguish hints of independence shown by the kulaks. Their supposed opposition to collectivization was translated in his paranoid mind into a nationalist uprising and plots to destroy him and the aims of the revolution. Victor Kravchenko, a communist agent assigned to keep the 1933 harvest from the mouths of those who had grown the grain, so that it could be exported, saw the consequences:

The most terrifying sights were the little children with skel-
eton limbs dangling from balloon-like abdomens. Starvation
had wiped every trace of youth from their faces, turning them
into tortured gargoyles; only in their eyes lingered the remains
of childhood. Everywhere we found men and women lying
prone (weak from hunger), their faces and bellies bloated,
their eyes utterly expressionless.   (Kravchenko 1946)

Under such circumstances they ate their livestock, their work-
horses, household pets, rats, mice, beetles, acorns, bark of trees,
grass – and then, it is said, each other. For obvious reasons, human
meat is nutritionally ideal for other human beings. Eating exhumed
corpses was followed, in some cases, by murdering in order to eat
the victim. Children, who were particularly vulnerable, were themselves able to overcome the taboo against cannibalism.

There are other examples of the final taboo being broken by
unbearable suffering. There is an oft-quoted story about the Warsaw
ghetto. A woman who jumped to her death overturned a cooking
pot with her falling body, "her blood and brains mixing with the
food". "Hordes of children, scrambling from their holes and cracks,
fought to eat the contaminated remains" (Russell 2006: 97). The
current famine in North Korea – largely due to a merciless regime
offering ideology and brutal repression as an alternative to any kind
of governance – is attended by rumours of the reduction of children to potential foodstuffs: to "special meat". To some this demonstrates that starvation promotes regression to an animal nature we
have not really transcended; after all, certain species such as horned
frogs are routinely cannibalistic, and some other primates in especially stressful conditions, as in captivity, may eat each other. But
what does this tell us about the nature of humanity and the extent
to which we have moved on from the condition of nature?

Perhaps the deepest and most impressive treatment of this question is to be found in Primo Levi's horrifying masterpiece *Survival*

in Auschwitz, where he describes from firsthand experience the Germans' "gigantic biological and social experiment" of the concentration camps. He wrote this book, he said, "to furnish documentation for a quiet study of certain aspects of the human mind". Given that Levi and the other prisoners endured not only hunger but also thirst, bitter cold, endless unbearably heavy physical labour, humiliation, illness and brutal punishment, with the ever-present threat of casual or planned extermination, and no hope of release, such documentation should command our attention.

The hunger was all-consuming, and could override everything, even fear or fatigue:

> The Lager [the camp] is hunger: we ourselves are hunger, living hunger …
>
> We have learned the value of food: now we also diligently scrape the bottom of the bowl after the ration and we hold it under our chins when we eat bread so as not to lose the crumbs. (Levi 1993: 33)

Prisoners try to position themselves in the soup queue to ensure that they are served from the bottom of the bowl, where what little nutriment there is in the filthy gruel will have settled. The dormitories at night are loud with the sound of inmates continuing to scrape the bottoms of their bowls – precious possessions that have to be guarded with their lives – in the hope of finding a few molecules of nutriment, and minutely examining them for overlooked fragments.

On first reading *Survival in Auschwitz* you notice what you expect to see: that many responded to the unremitting cruelty of the situation in which they found themselves by doing whatever was necessary to survive – stealing, currying favour with those who had power, ignoring the pleas of their dying fellow prisoners and shunning those who looked fated to die. On subsequent readings you notice other things.

There were acts of great kindness, self-sacrifice and incredible courage performed by those who were utterly destitute. Some prisoners managed to maintain an air of hope and authority that encouraged others. Others tried to keep up standards of a sort. A First World War veteran explained why he insisted on washing in the filthy water of the washroom:

> that precisely because [the camp] was a great machine to reduce us to beasts, we must not become beasts; that even in this place one can survive, and therefore one must want to survive, to tell the story, to bear witness; and that to survive we must force ourselves to save at least the scaffolding, the form of civilization. (Levi 1993: 41)

And even more astonishing was the intricate and complex infrastructure of theft and barter by which those who might otherwise have died survived. A few fragments of potato lying at the bottom of the soup ration are exchanged for a piece of bread or a rag of cloth passing for a shirt, a process that continues until the prisoner is exhausted or brutally beaten by a guard for breaking the rules. Even in the face of utter privation, food remains a commodity: something that has been humanly transformed from the nutriment that in animals merely maintains "a particular dynamic equilibrium".

Kindness, refusing to be degraded to beasts, wanting to bear witness and trading one's way out of certain death: this is not the way of beasts. Nor was the behaviour of the guards. Their own survival did not depend on the million petty and monstrous acts of brutality they carried out every day: they were driven by ideas, by convictions, that no animal could entertain. The hunger came from the fact that, as Max Litvinov said, "Food is a weapon". No animal uses food in this way or cruelly apes natural catastrophe. For human beings are alone in collectivizing the essentially solitary physiological experience of the need for nutrition in starvation, as a means of asserting and maintaining power. And while those who administered the camp system wanted to destroy those who suffered in it, either physically or as human beings, they still retained a margin of guilty awareness of their evil. That was why they wanted to ensure that no one was left to carry to the world "the evil tidings of what man's presumption made of man in Auschwitz" (Levi 1993: 55).

Hunger in Auschwitz remained profoundly human, as human, alas, as the evil that brought it about. Both the goodness of certain prisoners and the evil of those who imprisoned them are human: as human as the complex accommodations of those on both sides of the wire who fellow-travelled with wickedness in order to survive. The knowledge of good and evil is confined to the explicit creatures that we, of all sentient beings, are.

I have laboured this a little because, for some, hunger seems to tell us what we really are. What happens to us when we are savagely hungry seems to be a kind of critique of all those aspects of ourselves we take pride in as human beings. The knowledge that one would fight to protect one's full plate while others have empty ones, that one would hoard food while others around one are dying – glossed as prudence – remains as a guilty shadow at the heart of one's self-esteem. It should not, however, be misread. The events in Auschwitz, in the Ukraine, in North Korea, are not evidence that we are animals. It does not demonstrate that the gap between ourselves and beasts is narrower than we thought, even less justify denying that gap. What we see under those appalling circumstances are human causes and human effects.

What we do when we are hungry is no more the final truth about human beings than the sensations of hunger are "the low-down" or "the inner truth" of the organic states of our body. There is no such low-down, no such inner truth, because our bodies seen as carnal material do not have experiences that are intrinsic to them, least of all social experiences. This is the central mystery of hunger and the pathway to its transformation in human beings beyond physiological need. It is worth emphasizing this if only because one of the most pervasive ideas of the present age is that civilization is only "a thin veneer" and this is supposedly demonstrated again and again by the relapse into "the law of jungle" under conditions of competition for scarce resources. Offshoots of Darwinism, such as evolutionary psychology, provide a theoretical framework for this kind of thinking.

In fact this view is entirely cock-eyed. If civilizations are so fragile, so contrary to the natural propensity of a putative human nature, it is difficult to understand how they arose in the first place and how they have been such a constant feature of humanity over the past 10,000 years. War is seen as potent evidence for the natural incivility of man and with "The Age of Hatred" – the first fifty years of the twentieth century, in which more human beings killed more other human beings in war than at any time in history – fresh in our minds, we may be inclined to the notion that we are as much part of nature "red in tooth and claw" as any other living creature. Actually, the message presented by the horrors of war, although they are real, is not all that clear. Wars are very unnatural, un-animal activities. Contemporary wars are declared by politicians and are matters at least as much as for the quartermaster as for the fighting soldier. The proportion of war service that is spent in violent activity and the time soldiers pass in states of bloodthirsty aggression is minute compared with the time spent in rather non-animal activities such as thinking about home, grumbling about pay and playing cards. And their occasion is rarely directly about basic needs such as food.

Nevertheless, the idea dies hard that we are always on the verge of regressing to the state of nature on the grounds that we have travelled such a short distance from that state. The truth is otherwise. The infinite complexity of the hinterland of dinner is enough to tell us that. And we have hardly begun on the journey that our enquiry into the metamorphoses of hunger will take us.

2. Hedonistic hunger: foodism and beyond

Eating for pleasure

Jeremy Bentham, the father and prophet of utilitarianism, famously opens his *Introduction to the Principles of Morals and Legislation* with an apparent statement of the obvious: "Nature has placed mankind under the governance of two sovereign masters: pain and pleasure. It is for them alone to determine what we ought to do, as well as to determine what we shall do" (Bentham 1907: 1). Rational individuals should so order their affairs as to pursue pleasure and avoid pain; and the aim of rational and just government, and its instruments such as laws, should be to optimize human happiness by making possible the maximum amount of pleasure and the minimum amount of pain. Hunger seems to provide the paradigm driver to rational behaviour: eating both relieves the pain of hunger and affords pleasure. Nature thus reaches into the very heart of humanity, so that even governments and their laws can have a natural foundation. And yet we should be on our guard. This is not only because the goal of maximizing overall utility, without thought for justice for individuals – so that it is deemed right to crush those who seem to stand in the way of collective progress – has had such catastrophic effects in the twentieth century, and would have done so even if the leaders who used the rhetoric of utilitarianism had not been blood-boltered kleptocrats, but also because there is much about human hunger that is remote from nature and is even anti-natural. And this, as we have already seen, is true even of the seemingly primordial hunger – for food.

The culinary experiences enjoyed by the human subject widen into a world of pleasures, and secondary hungers and emergent needs that are only tangentially connected with the needs of the organism and the appetites typically associated with organic necessity, although they may be just as imperious. That the transformation of metabolic disturbances and their correction into painful and pleasurable experiences is an unexplained mystery should discourage us from taking for granted, or from seeing as "natural", the pursuit of pleasure, even in this seemingly most "natural" sphere of our human existence. *Pace* Bentham, there is much that is remote from nature in those two "sovereign masters" pleasure and pain, even when their cause is something as seemingly basic and natural as the need for food. While we may map some of our behaviour onto the pleasure-seeking and pain-avoiding tropisms or instincts of beasts, we have to remember that the latter do not have either particularly in mind as primary ends. And the strange – indirect, delayed, protracted or even perverse – pleasures that occupy us have no counterparts elsewhere in nature. As Kass has observed, the emergence of pleasurable intermediate activities between need and its satisfaction, means that these activities "which were originally adapted to serve nutrition and mere survival, eventually acquire a life and fulfilment of their own; they become part of the goal – as well as the means – of surviving" (Kass 1999: 88). This gap between need and its satisfaction grows wider, and is able to accommodate activities that have nothing whatsoever to do with survival and may indeed threaten it.

Speculating about animal consciousness is usually unwise. Those who do not fall into the Cartesian trap of assuming that beasts are insentient machines are likely to make the opposite error of anthropomorphism, attributing to beasts sensations, perceptions, beliefs and sentiments for which there is no unprejudiced evidence. There is a middle position that argues that animals do experience their own bodies – although not (as we shall discuss in the next chapter) as *their* bodies offset from the world and belonging to them – but that those experiences are unimaginably different from ours. We may draw some conclusions as to what it is like "in there": a whimpering, starved dog is probably suffering. Observation of animal feeding makes it reasonable to suspect that human beings are the only animals who truly *relish* their food, although non-human animals may feel the brief pleasure that comes from the relief of hunger. Worms seem unlikely to lick their stomata in anticipation of another helping of leaf mould. Relish also seems absent in the higher reaches of the animal kingdom. The cow consuming a day-long single-course meal of grass; the seagull swooping, snatching at fragments of bread, while fighting off the competition; the dog bolting pet food, the wolf wolfing down carrion – they all seem bent less on pleasure than on getting as much food inside themselves before it runs out, or is stolen. They are not Epicureans and seem unlikely to sign up to a Slow Food Movement. They give little indication that they *savour* what is in their mouths before it disappears into the dark interior of their bodies and is transformed into energy, order, tissues.

The full development of appetite and the foregrounding of pleasure ultimately owe their origins to biology, although they provide a springboard away from biology. Kass points out how in human beings certain developments, in particular the liberation of the mouth from a prehensile role and its elevation in upright man above the ground, are important precursors of the hedonistic approach to food:

the organ of ingestion acquires functions and pleasures of its own – biting, chewing, swallowing – as well as its own gustatory predilections and delights, which are logically, physiologically, and experientially separate from the ultimate goal of nourishment. Because it is such a long way from the taste buds to the true ports of call, food to the mouth need not be foodstuff to the intestine. The tasty or appetising and the fitting or needful – each at the heart of one of two possible definitions of food – need not be identical.   (1999: 23–4)

This anatomical separation of duties of course precedes human beings; but it is developed in man to the greatest degree and is so against a background of awareness and self-awareness, in particular of a uniquely complex oral awareness. Only under extreme and terrible circumstances do human beings eat like animals. Levi describes how in Auschwitz the guards spoke of the manner in which the prisoners ate as "*fressen*" rather than "*essen*": "this way of eating on our feet, furiously, burning our mouths and throats, without time to breathe ... [was] the way of eating of animals, and certainly not ... the human way of eating, seated in front of a table, religiously" (Levi 1993: 76).

For human beings living above subsistence, the relief of hunger is but a small part of the story of the pleasure of food, which, even at the level of sense experiences, is very complex. Taste is important, although it is only the ground floor. The receptors on the tongue report salt, sour, bitter and sweet and savouriness or umami and combinations thereof. These enable us to classify foods, and ensure that we are attracted to things that are truly nourishing and avoid those that are toxic. Much of the pleasure of food is attributed to smell, as anyone with a cold who cannot differentiate turnips from apple can testify. The range of smells, corresponding to different odorant molecules, is vast, and the receptors that they lock into are switched on and switched off during life. Complex scents – the aroma of meat immersed in gravy – are built up from the combinations of odorant molecules, like olfactory chords.

Flavour is constructed out of more than taste and smell. Texture is important. The crumbliness of apple crumble, the crunchiness of celery, the dissolution of things that "melt in the mouth", are all mediated by intra-oral touch. Even sound may be important, speaking texture out loud, as in the squeak of fried cheese and the gravel path crunch of celery. The fizz in fizzy drinks combines both tactile sensation and sound. Temperature also contributes to bringing out flavour. And there is the additive effect of flavours: the gravy on the potato, the marriage of meat with two veg, the entry of the pudding into a mouth still humming with the flavours of the food and wine already taken. Flavour is also influenced by the look of food, tuning our anticipations. When we taste an orange, we taste the *colour* orange and all the connotations this brings. And the layout on the plate or the structure of a cake exert their influence at least in part by how they look before we eat them as by the conjugations they make possible in the mouth. Vision brings with it its own set of memories that shape the anticipations that will judge the experiences released when the foods pass the lips. Memory itself is also very important. We may taste fragments of our past, even whole worlds, as the food releases its ensemble of sense experiences. Those memories, often more profound for not corresponding to precise events or clear images, soak the mouthful in a sauce of past days.

And this is just for starters. The experience of food is hugely influenced by our attitude towards what we are eating. Our knowledge that it is expensive, rare, cheap, possibly off, produced by an expert or by a tyro, that it is a gift or rather overpriced, may impact on flavour. There is top-down cognitive control of the oral experience that may tell us (to vary the old joke about Wagner's music) that it tastes better than it tastes. We learn to relish foods that on first encounter are quite disgusting, their pongs and sliminess reminding us of some of the least attractive aspects of our fellow human's bodies. Who would spontaneously relish a cheese that smells like a mixture of baby vomit and unwashed adult feet? Ambience is important: the way the table is laid, the temperature and lighting of the room, the absence of loud music drowning the flowers of conversation with the Paraquat of bass beat, the way the meal is orchestrated. The pleasure of eating is not easily separable from the pleasure of an occasion: the sense of collegiality, of celebration, of togetherness. In many cases food is subordinated to the wider social significance of the meal, an occasion that is a dense weave of events and experiences that mean something other than themselves. As Kass says, "we sow the seeds of community in breaking bread together" (1999: 131). The very word company is derived from *panis*, "bread", and *com*, "together". For some, feeding others, food as a gift, brings intense gratification: filling others' stomachs may be as joyful as filling one's own.

It will already be evident that we have the basis for a combinatorial explosion of possible culinary experiences and the material for a lifetime of gastronomic adventures. The importance of this becomes evident when we consider how much time, effort and thought is devoted to prolonging the pleasure associated with eating.

Prolonging the pleasure: the cultivation of appetite

Sensuous and symbolic pleasure become increasingly important as hunger is less intense. I am sure I speak for many when I say that I cannot last recall when eating was at the end of a period of hunger; when breakfast actually broke a fast. Hunger is rarely more than "peckishness"; typically, we look at the clock and decide that it is time "for a spot of lunch". Our children might complain that they are "starving" and I might say that "I could eat my way through a flock bed" but these are conscious exaggerations. Even when they are not, by the time we have reached the second course, hunger is less relevant as a driver to eating than habit, decorum and the sense that we need to stock up inside. By then we are concerned to pace our eating so that the edge is retained on our appetite.

In most cases, however, the law of diminishing returns seems to apply. Even before satiety is reached, and the signals from the full stomach switch off appetite, pleasure starts to wane. The second mouthful gives less pleasure than the first, the third less than the second, and before long one is just "finishing up" in order to be released to try the next course. At the most basic level, this is a reflection of the phenomenon of accommodation in the nervous system. The neural response to a stimulus fades when the stimulus is sustained or repeated. This is because we are tuned to be more aware of novel or changing stimuli than of those stimuli or states of affairs that are constant. Jading of appetite is many-levelled: the sensory nerves mediating taste and smell and texture are damped down; the sense of novelty becomes blunted; the excitement of the occasion subsides.

We do not, however, accept the properties of our own bodies, even those that we enjoy, as fixed and unalterable. Alfred North Whitehead observed that human beings are the only creatures who cultivate the emotions for their own sake – hence art. But it is equally true that we, uniquely, cultivate our appetites for their own sake. Led by the small minority throughout history who can take for granted a regular supply of adequate food, human beings have developed innumerable strategies for prolonging the pleasure of food. The simplest is to nurse our appetites, or so order our affairs that we do not spoil them: "hunger is the best sauce".

We also cook and variously process food and requisition its components from far and wide so that we can make our diet ever more varied and complex. Man is the most omnivorous of all animals. We want experience for its own sake and, after a time, quantity is not enough. The gourmand with a jaded palate becomes a gourmet, seeking an ever greater range of foods that commend themselves as "specialties", "delicacies" and "rarities". Some of these, like the cheese just referred to, will not be immediately attractive – either in prospect or in the mouth – and the notion emerges of the "acquired taste". The "difficult pleasure" is a pleasure prolonged in part by being postponed, by being rendered up slowly: we have to teach our bodies to be pleased by sensations that are initially uninteresting or outright disgusting. Indeed, a remarkable amount of acquiring taste is overcoming disgust: its residue adds savour to the food. There seem to be few natural constraints on what can be eaten with what. While Dame Edna Everage's recipes – "oysters in condensed milk", "fried truffles in wombat purée" – do not catch on, other pairings that may seem equally transgressive, such as fish and kiwi fruit, or deep fried Mars Bar, are acceptable to more mouths than is good for the bodies they feed. At any rate, the scale of our omnivorousness, unmatched in the animal kingdom because greatly enhanced by the processing of food, the sourcing of food from a range beyond that patrolled by any other creatures, and the testing out of limitless ways of combining foods, is a marker of what Kass has underlined: the unique openness of the upright animal to experience.

The gourmet may also seek to enhance enjoyment by serving his food in a rich gravy of lore, of expertise and of erudition. This is food with footnotes, giving the reasons why the experience yielded by eating it goes far beyond the simplicities of taste. We eat ideas, provenances and the vaunted skills of celebrity chefs so that, again, what we eat tastes better than any taste it may have. Associations, connotations and ideas insinuate themselves into the very substance of the stuff piled on the plate. This is true not only of gourmet dishes but of instant and fast food. There is plenty of evidence that branding makes food taste better: knowing that such and such a product is a particular brand can make it preferred over Brand X, even though the latter is deemed to be tastier in a blind tasting. The power of words over the palate is extraordinary. No wonder the national dish of America is the menu. The validity of this half-truth extends beyond the transatlantic world where waiters demonstrate their virtuosity by reciting the bill of fare without notes and thus enabling the food to come to be tasted in the "space of possibility", to be enjoyed as an abstract taste-in-the-head, prior to anything entering the mouth. As we progress from mere nutriment to *cuisine* and hence to *haute cuisine,* so enjoyment becomes more reflective.

When food is combined with wine, the subtle matching of drink to the food it counterpoints opens up a further combinatorial explosion of possibilities. There is no shortage of expert advice as to appropriate food and wine combinations – puddings, cheeses, starters, main courses – to go with red, white and pink wines. The acquired taste, the cultivated palate, of the wine drinker, is the supreme expression of ideas-in-the-mouth. It can develop unconstrained because wine corresponds to no primary need: it is a pleasure unanchored in physiology. The process of fermentation – by which the sugar in grapes, whose biological purpose was to attract birds that would then broadcast their seeds through their back passages on to the awaiting soil, is transformed by yeast into alcohol that transforms our outlook on the world – is a miracle; but it is as nothing to the miracle by which alcohol and the vehicle that carries it is metabolized to adjectives and, indeed, to long paragraphs of prose at once technical and enraptured:

Coteaux de Layon Beaulieu, Les Rouannieres, 2001 Chateau de Pierre Bise, Loire, France. This wine is so special – it is mouth-coatingly exotic, tropically fruity, long, smooth, and honeyed, with a glorious finish and a last lick of acidity to freshen the palate ...   (Jukes 2004: 159)

It is worth reflecting on just how far this takes us from the primary experience of food. Unpacking the tastes within one's mouth, using such concepts as "tropically fruity" and "mouth-coatingly exotic", suggests that the oral cavity has become a way station between the brain and a very complex world. The kind of introspective focus on sensations that could discover the notion of the "exotic" and the experience of the "tropical" on the tongue is unthinkable in organic or physiological terms. The tutored palate tastes distant places, abstract ideas, provenances, ambiences, social stations and its owner's standing in the world.

The ability to taste tastes in a certain articulate way – to identify, describe and evaluate them – becomes evidence of the kind of person one is. Reflective oral experience is connected with more abstract orders of awareness, self-awareness and social being. The tastes one has become a measure of how one ought to be judged. When John Ruskin said that "Taste … is the only morality. … Tell me what you like and I'll tell you what you are" he was not writing a motto for wine buffs or foodies but reminding us (albeit inadvertently) how the notion of taste, which has its origin in the refinement of appetite, and is ultimately rooted in primary experiences, reaches far beyond them. The experiences we have in the privacy of the mouth have a huge social surface. As Jeremy Iggers has put it: "Gastronomic 'good taste' … is the taste of a particular class of people, who have acquired a set of cultural resources. What we call good taste is just the taste of the dominant social class" (2007: 94).

Practices of consumption "reinforce distinctions in social class", for example by affirming the supposedly more refined sensibilities of those who live by their brains rather than their hands. This is the class that wishes to distance itself even further from instinctive and immediate pleasures by asserting a good taste that may not be based on what tastes good to the uninitiated. The connoisseur savours not only his food but also himself, or what his taste in food tells him about himself. And this in part explains the extraordinary power of branding: the link between taste and personal identity; or, rather, between professed taste and asserted personal identity.

Much of the life of those of us who live well above subsistence levels consists in pursuing goals that are proxies for primary hungers that are too easily satisfied. Our pleasures drift further and further from the incidental sensations associated with meeting physiological need. Even where those needs seem to be their ultimate object, as in the life of a foodie, much of the pleasure is to be found in the many intermediate steps. The moments when the food is inserted into the mouth and savoured are few compared with those spent happily reading cookbooks and trying to follow their instructions, or watching celebrity chefs on television, attending cooking lessons, or talking about food and swapping recipes. We ruminate not food itself but the processes that are involved in choosing, planning, preparing it. Food becomes word-riddled.

In short, while taste may have its physiology, taste soon becomes an all-pervasive preoccupation that has only a toehold on physiology. We may seem to be most obviously organisms when we are engaged in stuffing our mouths, but many of the pleasures of the table are remote from organic existence. The gap between ingesting food and having a meal encompasses much that is distinctive about human consciousness. The great distances opened up between the imperative to eat and the pleasures of the table tells us that these latter are far from primordial. While it is tempting to think, as Bentham did, that, like other animals, we are primarily motivated to seek pleasure and avoid pain, nothing is as straightforward as it at first seems even when we consider the immemorial, pre-cultural phenomenon of hunger and its satisfaction.

Theory-led eating

Our mouths are filled with words as we eat and relish our food, even if we do not speak with our mouths full. Our tastes are woven with theories. This opens on to a large topic that is currently preoccupying large numbers of people in the developed world. As a way into this topic, it may be instructive to look sideways at another fundamental trait we share with animals: energy conservation.

All animals so order their affairs as to minimize the energy expenditure associated with activity. In human beings, the self-selected walking speed closely matches the velocity that minimizes the metabolic cost. But for us that is not the end of the story. We often enjoy energy consumption for its own sake and there are circumstances, for example in the gym, where we aim to maximize metabolic cost in order to promote our future fitness. What is more, those activities in which we economize on energy expenditure by means of adjustment of velocity of gait are, for the most part, utterly unlike those in which animals participate: walking to work, attending evening classes, meeting to plan a holiday and so on. We often needlessly complicate our lives, and consume energy, in pursuit of pastimes and other diversions. Finally, we have found ways of conserving energy that have little to do with setting an appropriate gait speed: domesticating animals to become beasts of burden, inventing wheeled and other vehicles to transport us over the surface of the earth, enslaving or exploiting our conspecifics and creating a variety of engines and machines to do our work for us. These are many times more effective ways of energy conservation than optimizing our gait speed and other biomechanical strategies.

It is equally instructive to look at one of the "sovereign masters" under whose governance, according to Bentham, nature has placed mankind: pain. While we instinctively avoid some painful stimuli and dangers associated with the possibility of pain, we have to learn to avoid many others. Much of this learning is mediated through teaching – warnings of various sorts – which is unique to human beings. Human beings are the only animals that actively teach their offspring and their fellows. What is more, the teaching is often cast in verbal form, rather than by demonstration. Pain is also pre-empted by the creation, through cooperative activity, of a world sheltered from dangers both natural and manmade. We have collectively created an external milieu that is as friendly to living tissues as the *milieu interne* described by Claude Bernard. Only human beings have a Health and Safety Executive. We individually and jointly so order our affairs as to make the world a less painful place.

As it is with energy conservation, and the avoidance of pain, so it is with other "natural" propensities, such as the drive to eat. Animals seek food and, as we have noted, may or may not be pleasured by it. For much of the time, human beings who live beyond subsistence levels seek out food with pleasure in mind, as a primary aim, and increasingly the abstract idea of health, and from this unfolds a much more complex story in which the cognitive and the social dominate over the biological and the physiological. We approach food through multiple lenses of ideas and conceptions. We eat because we are hungry; but we also eat food because it will do us some kind of non-specific "good". That is why we are enjoined not only to eat but also to "eat up", to aim for a clean plate.

The most immediate good this does is to please, or to avoid displeasing, the person who is encouraging us to eat up. Thus did I, as a child, in response to maternal concern and paternal authority, force myself to swallow bacon rind as it was "the most nutritious" element of the material on the plate. It did not make my hair curl (as promised) but it makes my toes curl now as, half a century on, I remember struggling with gristle that seemed to reawaken some primordial disgust. And we eat up to demonstrate to our host how much pleasure her food has given us. Or we close our eyes and polish off the unspeakable delicacy cooked especially for us, honoured guests, when we have fallen among generous and prideful strangers in a strange land. The good the food does is that of gratifying others, by accepting their gift, accepting them. When I eat the food you have offered me I affirm my acceptance of you. I have assimilated you into myself. That is why "picky" eating can be construed as a moral failing. It is also at odds with that openness to new experiences that is part of the distinctive glory of mankind. And, as Matthew Brown has argued, "When you refuse to share food with others and make it a positive experience, you close off one of the central ways of connecting with other people in everyday life" (2007: 202). Spurned food is a symbol that runs deep: the refusal to break bread along with another is a rejection of that person, their culture, their self.

When we eat we send out to others signals about ourselves. The connoisseur relishes his *persona* – an individual of discernment and good fellowship – as well as the stuff on the plate. Ritualistic eating – turkey on Thanksgiving Day, carp on Christmas Eve – affirms our collective identity. Roland Barthes, in his deliciously mocking essay on "Steak and Chips" (1973), teases out the multiple symbols emitted by those who eat this patriotic combination: among other things, they are saluting La Belle France just as those who rejoice in the roast beef of Olde England give a friendly nod to Olde England: an England of a past whose pre-industrial charm is signalled in the "e" in "olde". Conformity to religious prescriptions and proscriptions on what food to eat when and with what is a mode of worship and a statement of membership of a group united in their deepest beliefs and values. The food we visibly eat, praise and advocate, and the eating rituals we respect, align us with a portion of the world that is larger than our body or the plate to which it is addressed. There are pressures to eat, therefore, that are remote from the hunger that is the experienced surface of physiological need: they come from the hunger to do the right thing.

This hunger also has roots in the suspicion that "you are what you eat". This is one of those irritating aphorisms that when you shake them, as Arthur Schnitzler said, shed a lie, leaving behind only a truism. Yes, what we eat is incorporated into the very tissues of our being. And food – its quantity, quality and kind – influences how we feel, what preoccupies us, and sometimes how we think. But there is much of us that lies beyond the reach of dietary influence. Even so, the desire to become the right sort of person by eating the right sort of food is one that has a hold on many people. We are suspicious that what we eat will turn us into something we would not like to be – for example a dead body. And not without cause.

We are equipped by nature to discriminate between food that is good for us and food that may do us harm. But nature has little concern for our life beyond the point at which we, disposable phenotypes, have ceased to do what evolutionary biologists would see as our essential business: securing the continuation of the genome by replicating it as many times as possible. In the natural state, longevity is not an intrinsic good and getting enough food to survive to replicate is the overriding concern. With the advent of affluence several things happen, as a result of which hunger ceases to be a reliable guide to our needs. First, we require less food as life for most of us becomes more sedentary and we have mere arias of set-piece physical activity as opposed to a recitative of grinding, aching, sweating toil. We have, therefore, to count our calories to make sure we do not translate a net energy gain into an ever-advancing state of portliness. Secondly, the efficiency with which we store excess calories as fat, while it is just what is needed when food supplies are intermittent and uncertain feast alternates with certain famine, is far from appropriate when food is in continued, guaranteed supply. Thirdly, since we now live longer, we have more time in which to harvest the long-term consequences of a diet that gives us more than we need. The result is a preoccupation with the relationship between chronic eating patterns and longer-term health.

Our eating consequently becomes ever more theory-led. A nation that is obsessed by food, when we no longer need to be obsessed in order to get enough of it, seems to divide its time between teaching itself more and more cunning and erudite ways of making nutrition a source of pleasure and of trying to regulate the eating of it; between being encouraged to eat more and being enjoined to eat less. At any rate, the meal comes shrink-wrapped in knowledge. In the midst of a plenty of cheap, energy dense foods, we count calories. We scrutinize what is on our plate with the eyes of biochemists, seeing not food but foodstuffs and nutrients, not meat but saturated fatty acids, not bread but "high carbs", not beverages but units of alcohol intake and E numbers. We eat "good" foods, like fruit and vegetables, to secure the prescribed intake; and the intake is unitized as "portions", portions that will guarantee us a reward in the short term of a conclusive bowel action and in the long term of surviving to see our grandchildren grow up. Our plates are piled up not just with delicious food but with potential consequences. We look past each individual meal and see a series of meals, summed in calculations by which we judge our intake against the recommended daily allowance, which has not to be exceeded on average, lest it be gathered up in our arteries as an alluvial deposit that will form the seed for thromboses that will bring our speech, our arm movements, our heart, our lives to an end; in short, deliver us to a death, not usually envisaged in biology, not from privation but from plenty. Our graves are dug more by our own teeth, ably assisted by knives and forks, than by those of predators.

Increasingly, as nations and their leaders become obsessed by the diseases of affluence, a polyphonic conversation intervenes between the forkful and the mouth for which it is destined. Evidence-based, evidence-lean, evidence-free, advisors make the dining table an *agora* where conflicting opinions slug it out. Indeed, those who talk with their mouth full may perform that routine miracle of using the same organ to ingest the food and to critique it at the same time. Every kitchen echoes with the guidelines that, generated by huge studies distilled by experts into simple and never entirely definitive advice, express the nation's collective concern with its own health as mediated by governments, usually and unfairly described as "states" of the nannying variety. Modest, and seemingly unenforceable, suggestions are characterized by those of a libertarian persuasion as coercive discourse inflicted on a cowed and bewildered people.

The classification of foods as healthy or unhealthy, and the category of health foods, go far beyond anything that we might learn from the sensations in our mouths, and they project both the eater and that which is eaten far into a future tense. The individual meal is a current account transaction while the sum total of meals is a kind of deposit account, often rather literally, as the succession of repasts leaves an alluvial deposit in the form of a filled out figure and a body mass index that will cause the owner, the partner or the physician to shake heads at a potentially diminished future. We are perhaps insufficiently astonished at how we have this sense of our own body's temporal depth, so that out of the succession of dinners we construct a temporal arrow whose flight describes an explicit passage from an explicit past to an explicit future with a certain life and health expectancy. What an egregious form of self-consciousness that can connect the meal I am eating today with the rapidity with which my non-existence is approaching me!

Beyond the rim of every plate, then, there is an open, largely invisible, space in which are camped a multitude of sciences, the great and not always consistent expert and lay community that uses them, and a long-term future of one's self and of the collective other. Increasingly, it seems, we live in a world not of stimuli or of material objects to be seized or avoided but of facts. (Why and how this is the case is connected with something very deep in human consciousness, and which we shall discuss in the next chapter.) The triumph of "the top-down" and the assimilation of food into discourse is ever more apparent. Although since prehistoric times the very processes of cooking the raw and sharing the resultant meals with others – one's dependents, one's neighbours and strangers – was pregnant with symbols, what is new is the extent of the domination of symbols over (relatively) raw appetite. In some, the symbols have achieved complete control. There are food faddists who eat their own ideas.

The perversions of hunger

The commonest eating disorder is simply eating too much, in particular of energy-dense foods such as chocolate, burgers and ready meals. The consequent pandemic of obesity has caused much alarm among those who are themselves overweight and those who are concerned with the demands the obese might come to make on health and other public services. In the US, approximately one-third of the adult population is obese and it has been claimed that eating too much of the wrong kind of food is a major contributory factor in half of all deaths. One British health minister argued that global warming was less of a threat than that of global becoming-globe-like. Whether or not this is true, a very significant part of the world's population is now more concerned with how to eat than how to get enough to eat. For many, dieting has become a way of life: starting it, sustaining it, breaking with it, discussing it, reading about it, seeking advice about, and help over, it. It is easy to make cheap points by comparing the lot of the first-world mother despairing that she has not lost the weight she gained during pregnancy with that of a mother in sub-Saharan Africa whose child has died sucking at breasts emptied by malnutrition. It is more instructive to think what this could mean; to consider the nature of the hunger that continues beyond the point at which the body should have signalled that its needs have been met and cried "enough". The explanation lies in the long chain of events and intermediate activities that intervene between the decision to eat or not to eat and the metabolic needs of the body.

We have already noted some of the more straightforward drivers to eating; that, for example, hunger is signalled by an empty stomach and other more subtle states of the body. The most obvious explanation is that filling the stomach switches off the signal to eat, hunger abates and the appetite goes. This is not the whole story, however, and some have argued it is not even a central part of the story.

Biological explanations have included low glucose levels, sudden rises in insulin levels (the hormone for regulating blood glucose), an increase in blood levels of fatty acids, mobilized as a result of starvation, and a fall in body temperature. None is satisfactory. They have been supplemented by theories of hunger and eating (and the latter, as we shall remind ourselves, may not require the former) based on learned responses to stimuli such as the smell, the sight, and the availability of food or on rather abstract "stimuli", such as catching sight of a clock reporting that midday has arrived. And finally there are cognitive drivers, which, as we shall discuss, assume increasing importance in a world where food supplies are assured. Among such drivers are those that have prompted me to drink several hundred cups of coffee and eat an equal number of biscuits during the writing of this book. The sense that it is "time for a break", the need to deal with a feeling of restlessness, the wish for an escape from intense activity that simply sitting still would not provide: such are the things that prompt contemporary man to eat.

It might be expected that hunger and satiety are in a simple relationship of opposition to one another: to be satiated is to be not-hungry. In the real mess of the real world, there are few direct logical oppositions of this kind. At the brain level, the signal to start eating appears to be influenced by a centre in one part of the hypothalamus and the signal to stop eating by a centre in another part of the brain. Satiety is more directly signalled by a full stomach than hunger is by an empty one. No wonder there is space in the case of the so-called vegetative function of eating for our behaviour to be idea-led. We do not stop eating when we are full, in part because the signal of satiety lags behind the objective fact of having had enough. We realize too late that we have eaten too much and for a few hours we are forced to be more corporeal than we would like: we are almost as much a stomach as we are when we are starving. Our solid, material existence oppresses us;

we are incarcerated in the state of our flesh, like a shell stuffed by the boiled egg within it. In those rare cases where we vomit, the feared vomiting when it occurs is a relief, liberating one from the state of plenitude, of being this body with these sensations, at once alien and deeply familiar.

One experience should be enough but it isn't. We are always in danger of overeating, if only because we cannot escape from the idea that if one portion gives pleasure, two portions will give twice as much pleasure and four portions twice as much again. Alternatively, we imagine that the delight of the first mouthful – or first drink – is infinitely repeatable. Even when we have direct sensory experience to the contrary, we cannot be disabused of this seductive idea. Sometimes the search is less for repeatable pleasure than for an imagined pleasure that eludes us. We eat a second orange in the hope that we shall this time taste the warm sunlight it promises, feel the colour orange in the mouth rather than the slightly acid sweetness we crush out of the slices as they die between our teeth, our palate and our tongue. The pleasure may be entirely in the idea – in the *anticipation*. I remember as a child looking forward all day to the Sunday evening roast dinner, my anticipation being wound up by the delicious aroma pervading the house, and then finding the pleasure I had looked forward to proving curiously elusive. Each mouthful was a mini-disappointment, that sent me on to the next mouthful in pursuit of the experience that eluded me. For Gustave Flaubert this was at the root of his commitment to art: "wine", he has his *alter ego* say in the early, unpublished version of *L'Éducation Sentimentale*, "has a taste unknown to those who drink it". That taste can be savoured only through art, a theme to which we shall return in Chapter 4.

Beyond those who routinely eat more than is objectively good for them, without being fully aware of it, there are those who are fully aware that they are eating more than is good for them, for their health or for the figure they cut in the world. And there are those who are clearly addicted to food. For foods addicts, enough is not enough; nor is a feast. Eating has become a compulsion that has broken free of the constraints of a hunger that can be satisfied. Instead of feeling helpless before a world of scarcity that does not meet their needs, they are helpless before their own compulsions in a world of abundance. The addiction may be as compelling as the primary hunger from which it takes its rise; the battle with nature to extract subsistence from it has been replaced by the battle with one's self and its hungers.

There are many and various explanations as to why food hunger should entirely break free of its moorings in physiological necessity or even ordinary appetite. Some will refer to low self-esteem due to lack of love in early childhood, and, linked with this, an obsession with body image that leads to a self-destructive urge. Others will focus on the chemical properties of the addictive substance. Chocolate, one of the commonest addictive foods, for example, gives pleasure owing to stimulation of the brain's opioid receptors, and the associated sense of withdrawal when the brain is denied its fix is uncomfortable. Yet other explanations focus on defective learning mechanisms: there is a low threshold for a stimulus, such as the presence or idea of chocolate, to lead to a response – reaching out for or going on the hunt for chocolate. An explanation that invokes the whole person will encompass all of these partial explanations. Such an explanation will take into account the fact that food has a huge and complex symbolic significance. Food after all is inseparable from our earliest and most intense relationships. Breastfeeding provides all forms of nurture at once; the refusal or acceptance of food is a way of refusing or accepting another person; and the giving of food is one of the most primordial of gift relationships. Food addicts are always making gifts to themselves, perhaps making up for a world that seems to withhold that emotional nourishment for which we human beings hunger almost as much as for nutriment.

Such addictions raise questions about the nature and limits of our free will. They illustrate, perhaps, the extent to which we create and undermine the conditions of our own freedom, individually and collectively. The cultivation of habits that support long-term goals that we ourselves desire "wholeheartedly" or "wholeselvedly" is one way in which we provide favourable conditions for the exercise of our freedom; and the cultivation of habits that undermine those long-term goals – by distracting us from them or making them more difficult to take seriously – erode our freedom. The addict is permanently preoccupied with the short-term goals of the next fix or avoiding the temptation to have or pursue the next fix. The horizon is lowered and matters of life and death or broader concerns for others are displaced by questions such as "Shall I risk going into the kitchen?" and "How will I re-route my journey so that I do not pass the sweet shop?" Questions of the ends and aims of life, great issues of state, the sufferings of others, are eclipsed by these petty preoccupations.

In short, food addicts live in a world that may be almost as shrunken as that of someone who is starving, although they may not be suffering as actively. This metamorphosis of hunger illustrates two things: first that the hungers we acquire when the primary hunger is met may sometimes be just as consuming; and secondly, our freedom from hunger, the very condition of other freedoms, may be squandered and we replicate in plenitude the prison of physiological necessity from which we have helped each other to escape. And this is illustrated by other more obvious addictions. When someone describes themselves as "gasping for a fag", this, although an exaggeration, captures the way the need for nicotine-bearing smoke has become as intense as the need for air itself. As the public health doctor Thomas McKeown once said, in a somewhat Calvinistic mood, "Our vices begin as pleasures we do not need and end as necessities that give us no pleasure". The addict has found a way of prolonging necessity beyond primary need.

The most spectacular food faddists are the bulimics who stuff themselves to bursting. This can be almost literally true, as I know from a patient who was admitted as an emergency to a hospital I was working at. She had eaten vast quantities of black pudding, sausages, potatoes, chocolate and much else besides. As a consequence, her stomach had become so distended that insufficient blood could pass through its over-stretched walls. This quickly infarcted and the rotting stomach wall released toxins that sent her into such shock that an emergency gastrectomy could not save her. Bulimics seem to eat to vomit. Erin Palmer, a recovering bulimic, described the ecstasy of her condition: "The whole purge process was cleansing. It was a combination of every type of spiritual, sexual, and emotional relief I had ever felt in my life" (Sacker & Zimmer 1987: 28).

At the opposite end of the spectrum to food addiction is food phobia – which can often be a life-sentence or, indeed a death sentence – and illustrates how information without perspective can be highly dangerous. Concern with avoiding toxic or infected foods generalizes to ill-informed worries about "chemicals" in food (as if all foods, and indeed those who eat them, are not chemicals), to notions of the "organic" that belong more to rhetoric than science, and to the fantasy of "the detox" in which "toxins" are cleaned out by "natural" procedures such as colonic irrigation and drinking bottled water. Anxiety about what is on the end of one's fork may escalate to the point where everything seems to be contaminated by chemicals or, for some, "germs".

There have been famous individuals who have died through fear of contaminated food, an egregious example of a fear bringing about the very thing it feared. Howard Hughes, the billionaire aviator and film-maker, became increasingly paranoid and reclusive through germ phobia. He spent the last years of his life in darkened hotel rooms which he believed had been rendered germ-free, wore tissue boxes on his feet, and burned his clothes if someone near him became ill. In the meantime, he starved himself, neglected every aspect of his own hygiene and effectively rotted to death. An even more striking example is that of the great logician Kurt Gödel who spent a lifetime in fear of accidental poisoning through his food. He was severely malnourished for most of his adult life, and in his later years became a recluse, emaciated, paranoid and hypochondriacal, and effectively starved himself to death.

The inability of the twentieth-century's greatest logician to conclude from the health of those around him that it was probably all right to eat the same food as they did is a startling demonstration of how food has a symbolic significance that lies too deep for syllogisms. It is, after all, something that we take into our own bodies and assimilate into what we, carnally, are. "The frozen moment when everyone sees what is at the end of the fork" that William Burroughs refers to in *The Naked Lunch* is not entirely comfortable. We are reminded of many things, the most important of which is that everything we eat is, or is derived from, life that has been destroyed. To the sensitized mind, satiety underlines something intrinsically repulsive – cruel, barbaric, laughably primitive – about eating. While the food miles and the processes and the rituals and the discourses that intervene between the killing of the beast and the slices of meat arranged tastefully on the plate sanitize the carnivorous state, some cannot help seeing the truth close up. They hear the off-stage screams of the living creature as surely as if it were giving up its life between their blood-stained jaws.

Fear of food may modulate into active hatred of it. Anyone who has observed from close up the spectacle of a young girl with anorexia nervosa starving herself to death will be in no doubt that, however fashionable the illness, however much it has been the focus of pop psychologists, this slow motion suicide, in full consciousness, in broad daylight, is an appalling tragedy. It has spawned an epidemic of theories. (According to Theory 17b, this is precisely the kind of attention people with anorexia wish to attract!) Here is not the place to review these theories in any systematic way – their sheer number betrays that none is satisfactory – only to reflect on the complexity of the relationships that are at work in such disorders.

There is the relationship to food: wanting it, feeling hostile to it, treating it with suspicion. There is the relationship to one's own body which is seen as being fatter than it really is. There is a relationship to special, or significant, others – parents, teachers, authority figures, important peers – to any individuals who exert control over one's life by seeming to define who one is by giving or withholding access to themselves. And there is a relationship to society at large, to that multifarious rumour of voices, images, theories, ocular and abstract stares and so on that seem to be passing judgement on one's body and the self that is and is not identified with, defined by, that body. This complex pattern of causation is matched by the Byzantine pattern of deception, self-deception and self-exposure that eating disorders involve. A person with anorexia will pretend to those who are concerned about her that she is eating enough, and then sneak off during or after every meal to the toilet to disgorge the contents of her stomach. The resultant cachexia broadcasts what is happening and this, in some respects, is what the person with anorexia wants. The worries she dismisses (and it usually is *she*) are precisely the ones she solicits. It is rather analogous to wearing dark glasses to hide tears and so broadcasting one's mourning.

Sheila Lintott has described how the person with a fully fledged eating disorder feels from within:

> You have never felt so alive and invigorated, have never before lived so purposively. Today brings the cherished opportunity to revert to the sublime hunger to which others succumb. You feel this way despite the fact that it is only a matter of time until your disordered eating makes an invalid, or corpse, of you. (2007: 59)

This last is no theoretical risk. Anorexia nervosa kills 25 per cent of those who suffer from it. While it may sometimes begin with an obsession with thinness and conforming to the stereotype of beauty, it soon changes into something quite different. The corpse-like appearance and the fetid breath of the hunger artist proclaims this. At its heart seems to be a desire to regain control. Nothing could be more impressive than the firmness of purpose and iron will of the anorexic. While her intermediate goals may be gaining respect and power, by redefining herself on her own terms, underneath this in turn is, Lintott argues persuasively, "the domination of the self over nature": "The eating-disordered individual locates herself in that part of her that is able to contemplate objects immense in size and to resist forces that threaten to destroy her: her hunger and her desire for food" (*ibid*.: 64).While it arises in response to a world "that conceives of a woman's worth in terms of her physical appearance … The eating disordered individual is engaged in a struggle, albeit a tragically misguided one, to demonstrate her strength and freedom and to win respect, especially from herself" (*ibid*: 69).

At this point it becomes more than an attack on being defined socially by one's body to an attack on the body itself, with its endless crude demands; a denial by the embodied subject of the fact that she is essentially, rather than merely accidentally, embodied; an attempt to escape the body as destiny. The episodes of bulimia to which anorexics are sometimes prone look like another way of mocking their own bodies. There is a connection – perhaps less clear and less self-evident than is often suggested – between anorexia nervosa and religious fasting; between the hunger for hunger and the hatred of the flesh, and a hunger for something that goes beyond the flesh and its endlessly renewed hunger.

Although in most cases the individual seems to be highly secretive, concealing her abnormal eating habits from others – particularly those who are most concerned for her health – they are, as already noted, a form of communication. The emaciated or grossly overweight body is a huge, standing sign or signal to others. The stick-like arms, or the apron of belly fat, are silent iterations that something is amiss; that the person within is at odds with the world. To use abnormal eating as a way of turning one's body into a sign, so that the flesh becomes something that both falls short of, and exceeds, a word, shows just how far hedonic pleasures may be transformed. Self-starvation may be a communication in another direction: it may be a way of interacting with an invisible world and invisible beings. The cultivation of hunger may serve what we shall, in Chapter 4, term the "fourth hunger".

From consumption to consumerism

According to the German philosopher Arthur Schopenhauer, boredom is inevitable: our lives oscillate between suffering, in which the will wills some end, and boredom, which comes as soon as that end is achieved. Boredom is a condition to be feared for it is a kind of toothless hunger – a hunger for hunger – in which it is life, rather than the stomach, that feels empty. Boredom seems like a truth, a window on to the ultimate futility of our lives, revealing the ocean of purposelessness into which the streams of purpose run. The most appalling feature of the abyss that yawns with our yawns is that it is only six inches deep, and says that we, too, and our lives, are equally shallow. While hunger is positive, its relief and the pleasure that comes with it are negative. This would explain why hunger can last so long as one does not have enough to eat – in some cases all one's life; while pleasure is ephemeral, hardly outlasting the moments in which hunger is satisfied.

Boredom is not as pervasive in affluent societies as Schopenhauer would lead us to expect because human life is infinitely more complex than it appears to the X-ray vision of the philosopher looking through the warm flesh to the cold bones. The roads that lead to the satisfaction of our needs are long and winding and involve many intermediate goals. There are innumerable steps between the pang in the stomach and the food on the fork. We have already examined some of them and also the ways in which the pleasures of the food on the fork may be prolonged, in part by making the journey towards them rich with secondary ends. More importantly, we develop other material or quasi-material needs that can under some circumstances seem as compelling as those of our primary hungers. The proliferation of needs and of the modes of consumption that answer to them keeps the abyss well hidden. By this means we may live in the shallows of physiological satiety in such a way as not to live or suffer its shallowness.

Blaise Pascal, a polymathic genius who died relatively young after a lifetime of physical and spiritual pain, was a penetrating commentator on this aspect of human life. One of the most sustained runs of the fragments in his *Pensées* is devoted to the notion of the *divertissement*: the diversion. He reflected on hunting, that all-consuming passion of many of his fellow men, and noted that the prize hardly justifies the chase. Twenty, thirty, men gather together, dressed, mounted and equipped at great cost, and spend a day or more chasing after a handful of unfortunate beasts, at risk to life, limb and property. The outgoings – the expenditure of time, effort and resources – are enormous yet the reward is meagre: a few deer, a hare, an inedible fox. If the benefit were understood in terms of the haul of edibles, the exercise would not stand up to a cost-benefit analysis: "if offered [the hare] as a gift, we would refuse [it]" (Pascal 1961: 84). The quarry is not the point of the chase, but merely its pretext, and the chase, purportedly a means to an end, is actually the end itself. Those who participate don't realize this: "They do not know that it is the chase and not the quarry that they pursue" (*ibid*.: 85). The reason the chase itself is prized over the quarry is that the latter "would not protect us from thoughts of our death and misery, but the chase, which distracts our attention, does so" (*ibid.*).

It is easy to recognize the contemporary truth of what Pascal says. Where his emphasis may differ from one appropriate to today's *divertissiers* is that he identifies fear of thinking about "death, wretchedness and ignorance" as the prime movers to the restless pursuit of distractions. Being less closely encircled by death for most of our lives, less exposed to evidence of our own wretchedness, and being more completely immersed in a soup of information that conceals from us our fundamental ignorance, we are more concerned perhaps to escape boredom. But Pascal's fundamental point remains valid. Those of us who are lucky enough to have our primary biological hungers – for food, drink, warmth, safety and so on – met, have to find other hungers. They cannot, however, be invented from scratch, otherwise they would command no authority over us: they have to at least have a toehold in those primary appetites. Hunting seems precisely to meet these requirements. The means to the end become sufficiently absorbing to be ends in themselves. One day, the fly fisherman will land that big salmon that may be tastier and more nutritious than any salmon, any fish or any food he could obtain by other means. For the present, however, he is content with secondary satisfactions: buying a new rod, making his own flies, arguing with friends about the best way of paying for a licence, swapping stories about fish that did or did not get away, planning trips and so on.

Of all the *divertissements*, organized, competitive sports are the most capacious. They seem to occupy much of the waking consciousness of a very large number of people. Half of the world's population anticipated, watched and debated the 2006 football World Cup. The discussions that surround the prospects and performances of a single club in a particular sport in a particular league in a particular country ramify without end. The investment of attention, preoccupation, physical effort, finance, organization, in the run-up to a contest whose winner will be barely remembered in the following year, is a staggering example of a prize not worthy of the chase. And it seems as if this multiform, hydra-headed preoccupation is appropriating a greater and greater proportion of collective human awareness, as the discussion moves further and further away from the central events – a goal scored – to arguments about ticket touts, about the behaviour of supporters, about the fitness of certain players, about the sex lives of the players, about the rivalry between managers and what they said to each other, about the interpretation of rules, about the use of video-playback in a particular instance and so on. The pointlessness of this, and similar, pastimes, evident to all but those who are caught up in the collective preoccupation, is irrelevant because they pass time. And, as time passes and we are propelled towards death at a seemingly ever-increasing speed (since time seems to be just as subject to inflation as money), they distract us from our end, and from contemplation of the rocky parts of the road towards our end, which might become too clearly visible if turbulence in our consciousness subsided.

The relevance of this to our theme of hunger is that the pursuit of pleasure and of distraction may follow paths remote from the direct elaboration or even the perversion of the joys of food or other biological necessities. The use of the word "consumption" to encompass many of the activities that fill the lives of the affluent betrays this sense of deep connection. In some respects it may also be misleading: much of what we call "consumption" involves items that are not consumed in the literal sense but rather are purchased and retained for use: so-called consumer durables. Nevertheless, there is a kinship between the pursuit of consumer goods and the primordial form of consumption, between shopping and stuffing one's mouths with nutriment. Keys's Minnesota experiment, which we discussed in Chapter 1, casts an interesting light on this. As the weeks went by, weight was lost, mood deteriorated drastically, and hunger became a permanent preoccupation. On excursions into town:

> the men sometimes went on shopping sprees, possessed by a desire to collect knickknacks, second-hand clothes, and miscellaneous junk. Afterwards, they were puzzled and dismayed: who would want these stacks of old books, this damaged coffee pot, this collection of spoons?
>
> (Russell 2006: 126)

There could be no clearer expression of the trade-off between, or symbolic equivalence of, eating and other forms of consumption. In the affluent parts of the world, consumer goods are more often what we eat symbolically when we have had enough to eat literally. Shopaholics may be in mourning for their lost appetites, seeking satisfaction elsewhere when their mouths and stomachs have yielded up all the pleasure they have to offer. These modes of consumption are therefore justifiably seen as modifications of the basic act of appropriation of the world: ingestion.

Man the Consumer is infinitely complex. Once hunger overflows the channels laid down by physiology and even loses direct contact with the body, and flows into that boundless space of possibility created by the community of human minds, it acquires a multitude of secondary meanings and drivers: the pursuit of novelty, curiosity, the desire to enlarge ourselves in our own eyes and that of others (whose most conspicuous manifestation is conspicuous consumption), the need to make ourselves feel safe, the necessity for gear, kit, caboodle, clothing and so on associated with activities that may or may not, directly or indirectly, serve our primary needs, and the mere continuation of the habit of consumption. The list could be extended indefinitely. The many layers of our possessions – primary necessities (such as shelter) elaborated way beyond necessity, secondary necessities that are necessary to make the primary necessities function properly, tertiary necessities that make the primary and secondary necessities looks beautiful, feel comfortable and be less demanding of labour – these are just the lower slopes of a hierarchy of possessions that culminates in out-and-out luxuries. Luxuries in turn bring with them their secondary necessities: those things that are required to make them safe, commodious, and deliver what we hoped. A yacht, a villa in Spain, a holiday in the Seychelles: all require a vast supporting cast of bits and pieces to make them work. The very world we live in demands that we consume many things beyond our bodily needs. Without emails, laptops, mobile phones, access to the internet, I could not have contracted to write this book and delivered on the contract. The very haste by which we have to consume things – to rush from pastime, to occasion, to spectacle – requires more consumer items of us, so that we can move more quickly. Taxis are necessary to get us from the theatre to the dinner, planes to get us from a bargain break weekend in a European city to a family dinner at home. Consumption that has to be hasty requires more consumption to enable us to keep up with the speed of the hedonic treadmill. The internal logic of consumption, by which it evolves towards an ever more inflamed state of consumerism, is powered to unfold in so many directions.

The hunting and gathering in of possessions becomes all-consuming (the word is unavoidable). Getting and spending, early and late, we are eaten up by the process of consumption. The replacement, refurbishment, upgrading, maintenance and protection of our possessions occupy an increasing proportion of our time. We are, as Nietzsche said, "possessed by our possessions". We are preoccupied by them, to the point sometimes of experiencing an anxiety that consumes us, that gnaws us from within. And, all the time, we are driven to redefine upwards the notion of "bare necessities" as our hungers become more remote from the body and its immediate needs, reaching further and further into an ever-expanding space of possibility. Indeed, we bitterly resent any retrenchment, echoing King Lear's famous rejoinder to his daughters' suggestion that, having given up his kingdom, he may need fewer retainers of his own, perhaps none at all:

> O, reason not the need! Our basest beggars
> Are in the poorest thing superfluous:
> Allow not nature more than nature's needs,
> Man's life is cheap as beast's ...
>
> (Shakespeare, *King Lear*, II.iv.264–6)

Even voluntary downsizing, in the direction of what is merely necessary, may seem an insupportable austerity. The most sincere downsizer may find the voluntary reduced circumstances unsustainable. The many communities in which we pass our lives make demands on us that require us to continue consuming at the same level as others: consumption on a scale unimaginable to most of our ancestors is the price of full membership of the various social groups to which we belong. For a child – who will experience the pressure of expectation and competition from peers more intensely through lack of inner resources and the deposit account of *curriculum vitae*, and will feel more completely and immediately defined by the "must-haves" she does or does not have – the most expensive trainers or designer label dresses will be "bare necessities" and that perception will be transmitted to her parents. If, as Spinoza said, "we desire that which we see others desire", it is in part because we are ourselves defined in the gaze of others by the extent to which we are desirable and our desirability seems inseparable from our ability to possess the fruits of the earth or, more precisely, of the human world. Possessions, what is more, are a means of vicariously possessing others, not merely by having what others want and dream themselves of possessing, but also because, as Marx pointed out, they embody the labours of others. This is the basis of that "fetishism of commodities" of which he spoke so profoundly in the first chapter of *Capital*: the mystery inherent in the fact that they contain a little of other human beings – their time, their labour – and thereby transcend their material properties.

Epicurus pointed out that "The wealth demanded by nature is both limited and easily procured" while "that demanded by idle imaginings stretches on to infinity" (quoted by Symons 2007: 25). Unlike the consumption of food, the consumption of consumer items has no natural limits. That is their attraction; on account of their infinite variety, they have a promise that fills the emptiness opened up by satiety. And the most potent agent of insatiable consumption, whether of consumer durables or of occasions, vacations, pastimes, sexual experiences, alcohol, or exotic food, is *money* – "frozen desire" – which is also a kind of commodity, a consumer item in itself. Much of our hunting and gathering is about the acquisition of money – the "wherewithal" – although what we gather is increasingly an abstraction, an idea, a quantized portion of frozen desire. What we collect is not gold, or even notes standing in for gold, but numbers on a salary slip, a share certificate, a bank statement.

Sigmund Freud argued that money did not bring happiness because it did not correspond to a prehistoric wish, but that is not quite the explanation. Prehistoric wishes – for food, fluid, warmth, shelter, sex – don't bring happiness either. The hunger for money is intrinsically unsatisfactory because it illustrates, more than any other acquisitive hunger, how, once one goes beyond hungers that are rooted in primary needs, consumption has no intrinsic ceiling. The person with £100,000 wants to be a millionaire; the millionaire wants to be multi-millionaire; the multi-millionaire wants to be a billionaire; the billionaire wants to be a multi-billionaire; and doubtless the multi-billionaire has his eye on being the first trillionaire. Inflation affects money; our accommodation to whatever we have, however, devalues money even faster than inflation. The most important thing about money is that it isn't really consumed: it is a mediator of consumption, a dry heap of abstract possibility, reduced to quantity. The nearest to money's being consumed is in the experience of the miser endlessly counting actual ingots, real coins, palpable bank notes, as he rubs his hands to put his physical presence to himself in italics. The act of counting, and re-counting, is close to consumption in a primary sense. It is certainly more real than the spending-under-anaesthetic of the credit card world and the subsequent post-transaction awakening when the bills are checked. It is not difficult to imagine how the love of hoarding, and the sense of enlargement that comes from accumulating tangible assets, might make the miser likely to neglect primary hungers; how his meanness might extend not only to others but to his own body, so that the hands he rubs together are skin and bone and numb with cold.

In many respects the miser is the prototype of all collectors: his collection is a collection of *possibilities*; indeed, it is a collection of second-order possibilities. For that which money can buy is itself conceived as the possibility of experience, of pleasure, of a mode of being. But perhaps it brings fewer rewards in the form of the satis- faction of secondary hungers, because in its purest form the accu- mulation of wealth is a solitary activity, the erection of a private monument or castle. Indeed, fellow beings, when they are not the means by which one might add to one's pile, are a threat to it. The miser's natural home is a safe; the world in which he lives is popu- lated by potential thieves. Other collectors – of train numbers, of stamps, of Meissen porcelain – are less solitary. Their acquisitive passion connects them with a community of fellow enthusiasts and, even though they may be competing for particular acquisitions and enviously comparing their collections, this opens up the possibility of intercourse with one's fellow men, even the formation of clubs and societies, where the collection, the collectable, and the ways to and barriers to collections, may be discussed *ad infinitum*. Clubs require rules, and meetings, and officers and strategic plans, news-letters, fund-raising events: in short, *divertissements* galore.

All of this demonstrates how far off the mark are those who try to naturalize the collectors' passion by comparing it to hunting and gathering. Leaving aside that the kinds of things that are collected – sightings of rare birds, postage stamps, train numbers, precious crockery that is to be exhibited but never used – are remote from the kinds of things hunters and gatherers hunt and gather, the organizational structures that we have alluded to hardly match those of the hunting pack or even the solitary predator. What is more, there is the distinctive goal of the collector: not necessarily to have the biggest collection but to have the best collection; one that is unique in its completeness, in the rarity or quality or antiquity of its items. A complete collection becomes a model of the world; or of the world possessed. If, as Lévi-Strauss says, the aim of mankind is "to make the world its thing", collecting – or at least the regulative idea behind it – is a faint echo of that fundamental aim.

Concluding thoughts

It is time to gather up the threads of the discussion. We began with the observation that man seems to be the only animal that truly relishes its food. For other animals, there may be the relief of the suffering associated with starvation but many human beings have so ordered their affairs that the avoidance of pain, the misery of starvation, is for most of their lives less important than the pursuit of pleasure. At any rate, in man alone does pleasure become a primary, indeed an explicit, aim. Once basic needs are met, and reliable food supplies are secured, human beings become preoccu-pied with sustaining, protracting, maximizing, that pleasure. The explicit gap between the idea of eating and the actual process – a matter of minutes or hours in cooking and days, weeks or months in agriculture – awakens a different kind of consciousness of food. The combination of regular satiety and an interval in which food is entertained as an explicit possibility, as an abstract idea, opens up a space in which the primary hunger can be transformed into a complex network of secondary hungers.

Unfortunately, notwithstanding the potentially infinite variety of foods, and the combinatorial explosion of possible food combinations, satiety is inevitable, and boredom, meaninglessness, threatens. Restaurant critics, for whom eating pleasurable food is a daily, indeed mandatory, experience, would seem to be at most risk from food anhedonia, but actually survive with their oral libido intact because they subordinate eating to work and have a responsibility to observe, articulate and judge, and because the act of attentively eating food is that by which they earn the money that gives them the wherewithal to pursue other projects. Without this, the pleasure of eating would turn into gastrointestinal drudgery. The hundreds of cookery books published a year, and their domination of the bestseller lists, is a tribute to the inexhaustible hunger the public seems to have for *discourse* about food.

The hunger for hunger drives the development of other hungers: for the enjoyment of acquired tastes, for the accumulation of possessions and for all those *"divertissements"* that Pascal spoke of. These hungers are not, of course, fuelled solely from within. There are seemingly internal drivers arising from the phenomenon of accommodation to a sustained stimulus, so that the pleasurable yields decreasing pleasure. And there are other apparently internal drivers based on the obverse of this: the recalibration of expectation and of what one is prepared to tolerate. This is enshrined in the story of the Princess and the Pea. But not all the drivers are internal. We make sense of our needs and translate them into necessities, and into hungers, in general terms: our needs are the result of an interpretation based on what is generally thought and said around us. This makes us receptive to the seductions of various agencies, the hidden and not-so-hidden persuaders, whose livelihood depends on making us feel new needs. In an exchange economy mediated by money, meeting the needs of one depends on awakening the needs of others. Where production is large in scale, the awakening of needs in others is mediated by the entire community of discourse. The great rumour that is the human world in which we individually live – or in which we individually carve our lives out of the collective – is incessantly reminding us of things we need and evoking a sense within us of their necessity. Where hunger cannot be awoken directly, it can be invoked indirectly through anxiety about our physical appearance, our social standing, our safety, our future prospects and so on.

This industry of hunger-creation was examined in great depth by philosophers and sociologists in the twentieth century – notably by such writers as Herbert Marcuse, Vance Packard and J. K. Galbraith – but it was anticipated long before that by Hegel in *The Philosophy of Right*:

> What the English call "comfort" is something inexhaustible and illimitable. Others can reveal to you that what you take to be comfort at any stage is discomfort, and these discoveries never come to an end. Hence the need for greater comfort does not exactly arise within you directly; it is suggested to you by those who hope to make a profit from its creation.
> (Quoted in McMahon 2005: 371)

While the primary hunger understood in its narrowly biological senses is incidentally social, the secondary hungers are increasingly social not only in their inspiration but in their expression. Collectors naturally collect themselves together into clubs where their passions may be shared and validated against a world that may not share them. Hobbyists seek out fellow hobbyists. The point is this: as we move from primary hungers to secondary ones, to longings and aches that owe a distant ancestry to the pangs of hunger that are being prolonged in order that satisfaction may continue throughout our life, so we move increasingly into a space of possibility, into a universe of ideas, into a shared human world of complex interactions. Our appetites, in short, become ever more riddled with, expressed in, words and, more generally, symbols and modes of communication. We have decisively left the solitary body of the comparatively mute sentient beast, where biological needs have their origin, for mediated experiences, for ideas, for the world of words; in short, for the community of minds. The obverse of the socialization of appetite is the appetite for socialization. At its heart is a unique human hunger: the hunger for others.

3. The hunger for others

Preliminaries

We have travelled a long way from hunger understood as the conscious surface of biological need or the conscious correlate of a gap between the state of the organism and a state that is more compatible with continuing existence. Unlike animals, we eat not only to feed our bodies but also in response to psychological and social hungers that may be as compelling as the biological archetype. In this chapter, we shall travel much further in this direction and readers may need reassurance that the author has not lost the plot. My defence for what follows is that the history of humanity is that of a gradual loss of a biologically prescribed plot. The latter will reassert itself under conditions of severe privation: primary hunger returns and the secondary accretions, elaborations and perversions and the metaphorical and proxy expressions of hunger take a back seat. But even then, as it returns with sharpened teeth, it does not do so in the guise of pure physiological need, as we noted when we reflected on Levi's account of the hungry in Auschwitz. Under the ordinary circumstances of life as it is enjoyed in the West, however, the biological story will remain muffled and new stories of new hungers emerge.

At the heart of this new plot is the displacement of appetite by desires, in which appetites have been transformed in ways that are of central significance to human life. In fact, we had already entered the realm of desire when, in Chapter 2, we examined the various activities and passions of human beings seeking to escape satiety and how they undertook projects – such as those of the collector – that introduce stories into daily life beyond the cycle of hunger–eating–satiety–hunger. The fundamental object of desire, and the focus of desires at their most intense, is another person. It may become a raging, gnawing hunger, a hunger that consumes us from within, a hunger whose teeth are not physiological sensations associated with physiological privation, but imaginings, images, thoughts, words. To understand such a desire, or at least to see it clearly, we shall need to look more deeply into the distinctive nature of our human hungers and, beyond this, into our human being.

One of the reasons why it is difficult to make sense of what the hunger for others wants is that it has such protean manifestations. Its most obvious, direct and intense expression is sexual desire, which wishes to access, to possess, another person through their body: through our effect on their body, through their effect on ours. Some, most notably Freud, maintained that sexual desire lies at the bottom of all our hungers for others – indeed of many other hungers, such as for power, for knowledge, or for completing projects (rounding off stamp collections, building cities) – and that all other expressions are secondary or mere substitutes. Others, such as Hegel, whose thoughts lie at the centre of this chapter, make the hunger for domination the primordial expression of our hunger for others. Both thinkers were right in this respect: they saw how the hunger for others encompassed the heights and depths of our being; that it drove much, perhaps most, of what is distinctly wonderful and distinctively horrible about human beings. And they are right in another sense: that this hunger is a metaphysical appetite that goes far beyond the physical needs that energise and shape animal existence. In the hunger for others, we see human beings at their most hungry and hunger at its most human.

The hunger for others – the need to be needed, the need to be admired, to be ourselves an object of others' longing, to dominate –

drives ambition, the relentless pursuit of self-aggrandisement through possessions, office and accolade, the hunt for prestige, standing, esteem, power, the ache for honours and the terror of dishonour; it energises the lives of those who have done most to shape our world for good and ill. And it is a hunger from which no one escapes, even if they do not act it out on a great canvas, even if it does not have publicly visible consequences. Few have lived lives entirely free of the longing for others, the desire to be desired by them; few have entirely avoided the poison of jealousy, the despair of rejection, the mildew of envy. Perhaps never to have experienced these things is never quite to have lived the human condition. There are some for whom the hunger for others occludes everything else. There are those who kill themselves out of unhappy love. There are those – usually women – "who love too much". They put up with brutal partners who abuse and humiliate not only themselves but also their children, sometimes to the point of death. Their need for the presence, attention and approval of this monster, whose love has come to define the meaning of their life, is such that it overrides even the fundamental instinct to protect one's children from harm. There are those who suffer humiliation, pain, degradation, for the sake of a love that consumes them. There are self-destructive infatuates whose desperate hunger for the object of their longing makes them absurd, reckless in pursuit, gripped by an unshakeable fantasy that, in the end, they are loved, that they are the chosen one and that all the evidence to the contrary is due to misunderstandings. Daily life, the newspapers, the arts and history tell us how the need for others that goes beyond companionship, cooperation – bringing humiliation in rejection, ecstasy in accept-ance – may be such that nothing else can matter, nothing else seem of value. Jealousy corrodes everything, subordinating the various-ness of the world to signs germane to a single preoccupation. Being discarded destroys appetite for life and for the things of life, even the basic necessities. And the ultimate rejection – albeit involuntary – of bereavement may make life pointless.

In short, this hunger for others – for their love, their attention, their body, their life – may be as destructive of happiness as chronic malnutrition. The reader may wince at this suggestion but the ability of fixated, unhappy love to eat someone alive is undoubted. Barthes talks about the "amorous catastrophe" in which the rejected lover feels that he is doomed to total destruction because he is in a situation that is "irremediably bound to destroy him". It is a "panic" situation, "without remainder, without return": "I have projected myself into the other with such power that when I am without the other, I cannot recover myself, regain myself: I am lost, forever" (1978: 48–9). It is almost as if the satisfaction of primary hungers in human beings has opened a great space in which a new hunger, in its way almost as terrible, can get a foothold. Even so, the reader may feel that further justification is still required for moving from hunger for food to hunger for other people. Surely the link between the two is only metaphorical and is not sustained at a level sufficiently deep to be described as "philosophical". Let me offer some observations that might or might not be persuasive, because ultimately it is a matter of intuition.

We have already noted how at the beginning of our lives, when the deepest impressions are made, and our world picture acquires its most fundamental structures, food and the presence of others are inseparable. We acquire nourishment, security, warmth and the first stirrings of a sense of self at our mother's breast, which, while it satisfies a primary, biological need, also becomes the first object of our desire and knowledge. By the time the twelve-month-old baby has been entirely weaned on to solid foods, the sense of the self, and of the other, has become well established. It is not necessary to accept the sometimes absurd, and usually evidence-lean, speculations of the psychoanalysts to see the inseparability of the hunger for others – the need in the first instance for the existential reassurance of the mother's approving presence – and the hunger for food. After weaning, the relationship, never entirely straightforward as anyone who has breastfed a baby or observed the process can confirm, gets more complicated. Being difficult over food is one of the most potent weapons of the tyrant-tot asserting power over its, inescapably anxious, parents.

The connection between hunger for food and the profound need for acknowledgement by others is sealed forever, although it may remain less apparent on the surface. It is there in the expression of maternal love through feeding, and overfeeding, the child. It is equally present in the rejection of maternal love experienced through rejection of food. The trade-off between longing for another and hunger for food is equally evident in the loss of appetite experienced by the adolescent falling passionately and perhaps unhappily in love, as if one hunger drives out another and they are at a deep level equivalent. It is present more pervasively and less explicitly in the way we human beings do not experience hunger as a solitary experience but face it collectively as a scarcity collectively endured. Food, even under such dire circumstances, carries a heavy symbolic, as well as metabolic, significance.

It is not by accident, therefore, or indeed as a result of a merely superficial analogy, that we speak of suffering the "pangs" of love, of being "starved" of affection, of being "sick" with longing for a loved one, of being "eaten up" with jealousy, of being "gnawed from within" by grief at the loss of another person, either through death or rejection. The jealousy that eats us up may awaken thoughts of revenge addressed to those who have discarded or displaced us and revenge is "a dish best served cold". While the anxiety, the grief, the joy, of the lover's emotions may unfold through words, in an endless conversation with himself and, in reality or imagination, with the loved one, it is also felt in the pit of the stomach. The prospect of seeing the loved one, or the arrival of a letter, sets butterflies aflutter in the stomach. Bad news leaves him "gutted". Thoughts, by the very fact that they are endless, seem to translate into a state of tense emptiness, a hungry hollow in the pit of the self. The unremitting concentration on the other person – the object of our unhappy love – bores through the stomach wall.

The connection between hunger for food and hunger for others – expressed not only in words but in the very repertoire of bodily sensations through which both are experienced – thus runs very deep. To understand a little more about what happens in these depths, we need to examine the difference, or the distance between, appetites and desires. Only then will we be able to engage properly with Hegel, our key interlocutor.

From appetite to desire

> "I think", said the Major, taking his pipe from his mouth "that desire is the most wonderful thing in life. Anyone who can really feel it is a king and I envy nobody else!" He put back his pipe.
>
> "But Charles!" she cried, "Every common low man in Halifax feels nothing else!".
>
> He again took his pipe from his mouth.
>
> "That's merely appetite", he said.
>
> (D. H. Lawrence, *The Virgin and the Gypsy*)

While there is a residual connection between human appetites and biological hungers, desire has no counterpart in animals. To make sense of desire and to see the deep gulf between desires, which are intrinsically insatiable, and appetites, which may in some sense be satisfied, we need to look into the nature of human consciousness. A desire is an appetite that has a story – albeit unfolding, evolving, fragmented – at its heart. It is a hunger that narrates itself and tries to make sense of itself. Through the sense we make of our desires, we make sense of ourselves. To desire, Henry Miller said, is not merely to wish; it is to know what one truly is. But it is also to *stipulate* what one truly is: to assent to part of one's self as being worthy to define one's self. Like animals we live our lives; but unlike animals, we also *lead* them and do so, setting aside accidents and uncontrolled events, in accordance with an idea of ourselves. Much of the difference between living our lives and leading them is captured by narrative: the stories we tell ourselves (and others) about what we are going to be, about what we have been. These stories are both individual and collective. I plan my personal future, narrating what I want to happen to me, what I intend shall happen to me. But the communities to which I belong also have a collective sense of their own future: of a direction defined economically, politically, culturally, theologically. The stories are also small-scale and large-scale; I plan on a small scale to reach a certain desired goal and on a large scale to live, or to have lived, a certain kind of life. Communities take precautions for their immediate future that define their goals and have an evolving sense of their proper destiny. In each case, there is an ill-defined feeling of identity rooted in a summarizing glance at the past: the biographical past of the individual and the historical past of communities. The division between the private and the public, the personal and the political, the individual and the communal, is not sharp. We are independent points of departure, making private choices, but we do so in a field that is at least in part collectively defined: we have a private "take" on a collectively defined world. The possibilities we project for ourselves belong to a loosely defined space of possibility jointly established with a constituency of our fellow creatures that extends indefinitely in all directions. By this means our instincts, our appetites, our basic needs are utterly transformed and become distinctively human.

Our lives, then, are riddled with stories. The importance of stories to our discussion of the metamorphoses of hunger is that they mark the point at which appetites become desires. To understand how deep this goes, it is necessary to reflect on what is distinctive about human, as opposed to animal, consciousness. I hope the reader will forgive a short digression on this difference; it is, I believe, essential to making sense of the way hunger is transformed in us. To understand the hungers that occupy most of the consciousness of those that live above subsistence we need to appreciate the extent to which we are creatures that, uniquely, *entertain explicit possibilities.*

Animals are organisms that, in some cases, experience existence: their own bodies and the natural world that impinges on them. What they do not experience is *that* they exist. They have no sense of self, or no sustained sense of self: no self-consciousness or no sustained self-consciousness. (There is evidence of fleeting self-awareness in non-human primates but it is not extended or elaborated into a sense of self.) Unlike human beings, they are not embodied subjects confronted by a world of objects that are experienced as existing independently of them. The world we human beings feel ourselves to be in is, by contrast, composed of an indefinite number of items that we intuit as transcending our experiences. I see that the cup I observe in front of me has invisible parts; and anticipate that it has other properties accessible from other viewpoints or by other people. To say that I feel that objects transcend my experience is to say that I am aware that no experiences could completely exhaust what they are, leaving no unexperienced residue. Undissolved into my experience, they are utterly other than me. This has two important consequences. First, objects are granted an existence in themselves. I am aware *that* they exist. And secondly, they are surrounded by an irreducible aura of possibility. Animal consciousness does not distinguish the Self (that which we feel ourselves to be, corresponding to the intuition "that I am") and the Other (which confronts us as that which we are not, corresponding to the intuition "that it is"); they are, as it were, dissolved in their worlds.

This is not the place to explain how we human beings came to be so different from even our nearest primate kin and the full extent of that difference. (The interested reader may want to consult my *The*

Hand [2003], *I Am* [2004] and *The Knowing Animal* [2005].) Nor is it necessary here to examine the elaboration of self-consciousness into a complex sense of a self, bearing the notion of an evolving personal identity reaching into a past and future, to a greater or lesser extent sustained through its conscious life. We note only that this is the basis of a life led, as opposed to merely lived; of the narrative-riddled and narrative-guided daily life of human beings. And we need only to note, without further discussion, that the granting of independent existence to objects, rooted in our intuition that they transcend our experience of them, has given rise to our sense of the intrinsic properties of the material world, of causal relationships within it. As a result we have collectively embarked on a programme of enquiry that has led to the massive cognitive monument that is human knowledge, whose most obvious product has been the technology that permeates every aspect of our waking consciousness, separating us from nature by an artefactscape in which we pass much of our lives, and which has had a huge impact on the way we experience, seek to satisfy, and transform our basic hungers. I want to focus on something that is key to human consciousness, arising out of the sense "that I am" and "that it is".

Animals are surrounded by material objects but do not confront them as objects that exist or are the case in the way that human beings do. We alone have an awareness "*that* such-and-such is, or is not, or might be, or ought to be, the case". The world that we confront, engage with, inhabit, is immersed in, encompasses, material objects (in part dissolved into the nexus of significance to which they belong) – and facts. The way the world is presented to us, that which makes it a world rather than a mere array of material objects, is overwhelmingly in the form of facts. Facts are most typically, but not exclusively, indicated by sentences that express propositions. Our interactions with the world, our experiences of it, that to which we are addressed, have an actual or incipient or propositional form.

Our awareness, in short, is a propositional awareness remote from the sentience of animals.

It would be absurd to think of human consciousness as wall-to-wall talk with itself and others. While words are all-pervasive in our waking hours after infancy, this is not the entirety of our consciousness. We may think of the lattice of propositional awareness being coloured in with sense experience; and much of our experience is not verbalized, being registered pre-verbally or implicitly. Even where it is verbalized, the inner discourse usually takes the form of mere fragments of articulation (as James Joyce illustrated so brilliantly in his novel *Ulysses*). However, propositional awareness is not merely a commentary on that of which we are aware by other means: it is central to our being explicitly a self in a world. And while it is most evident in our utterances, it is also present in a multitude of other so-called "propositional attitudes".

"Propositional attitude" was a term introduced into philosophy by Bertrand Russell. It connects two notions: that of an "attitude" with that of a proposition. A *proposition* has the form "That X is the case"– or "might be made the case", or "ought to be the case", and so on. It is a proposed state of affairs, located in the space of possibility to which we referred. The *attitude* is the relationship the subject has to the proposition: knowledge, thought, belief, fear, desire, hope and so on. Typical propositional attitudes would be my knowledge that X is unwell, my fear that X is unwell, my belief that X is unwell, my hope that X is unwell and so on. Much of our consciousness takes the form of propositional attitudes, which may be regarded as crystallizations out of the super-saturated solution of propositional awareness.

There are two features that all propositional attitudes have in common. First, they are intentional states: they have *aboutness*: they are about a state of affairs, or something that is or might be the case. Secondly, they are directed to something *that exists in the space of possibility*: their targets have general characteristics, with features that are indeterminate. My belief, for example, that there is a cat in the house leaves undetermined where the cat is, what sort of cat it is and so on. This is even more obviously true of my belief that "Things are going to get better", or that "Someone is plotting against me". Unlike perceptions of objects, which also have intentionality, that which they are about is not located in space and time or in relation to the body of the believer. This is clearly true of false beliefs, even simple ones related to matters of fact: my incorrect belief that K2 is higher than Mount Everest or that it will stop raining in ten minutes obviously has no place in the material world around me. K2 has a place in the material world but the relation of its size to that of Mount Everest does not; nor does the belief that picks out this fact. It is destined to remain forever unactualized in the space of possibility. The intentional objects of propositional attitudes are free-floating. Even when, say, a belief is proved to be true, the state of affairs that proves it true is only one out of an indefinite number of realizations.

Philosophers talk about propositional attitudes being "satisfied"; for example, my belief that there is a cat in the room will be satisfied if there is indeed a cat in the room. The neat fit between the propositional attitude and its satisfaction conditions is, however, deceptive. The one seems to fit the other – like a tautology fitting itself – only because both are cast in words; that is to say in general terms, there is the same level of generality in the conception of that which has to be satisfied and that which satisfies it. In reality, satisfaction is incomplete because there are many other states of affairs that could have satisfied the propositional attitude, as the latter proposes an indefinite range of possibilities. That propositional attitudes cannot be completely satisfied, that they are "unsatisfyingly satisfied", becomes important when our appetites (which are not articulated to themselves) are replaced by desires (which are). The word "satisfy" means, etymologically, "to make enough". Hungers in the form of appetites can achieve satiety because "good enough" is "enough": anything corresponding to what is needed is good enough. It matters less that my hunger is satisfied by a tasty ham sandwich rather than by a tasty chicken sandwich than that it is satisfied. Good enough is all that is needed for relief from the discomfort of unmet biological need. It is, however, not enough for those propositional attitudes that reach beyond need and practical necessity. I am perfectly satisfied when my belief that there is a cat loose in the house is confirmed by a particular encounter with a particular cat in the house. I am equally satisfied when my wish (hope, intention) that I will arrive in London at a particular time is fulfilled in a particular light I had not envisaged. Desire that goes beyond practical necessity may not be so clearly satisfied. The mismatch between the desire and any particular realization becomes important. This has particular salience when the object of our desire is another person. While needs may be met and appetites extinguished by satisfaction, non-instrumental desires are intrinsically insatiable. No particular man can satisfy the desire for "a man"; and no particular interaction with a particular man can satisfy the desire for that man. For this reason alone, there would seem to be something potentially tragic in our desire for others.

The tragic nature of our hunger for others has preoccupied many artists and thinkers. The course of true – and untrue – love rarely runs smooth. What has interested philosophers is whether it ever could do so. I have suggested a reason why our hunger for others is intrinsically incapable of satisfaction. Others have given more dramatic reasons why this hunger should bring suffering. Among them are two of the most influential philosophers of the past two hundred years: G. W. F. Hegel and Jean-Paul Sartre. Hegel's views are some of the most profound thoughts in the Western philosophical literature, although they are virtually buried in the opaque prose of his first major work, *The Phenomenology of Spirit*.

Hegel – and Sartre

> for each self is the enemy of all others and would like to tyran-
> nise them. (Pascal 1995: 597)

Hegel was not the first to remind human beings that they differed from all other sentient beings in virtue of being not only conscious but also self-conscious. But he arrived at some compelling conclusions by reflecting on this difference. Conscious beings have a sense of lack that can be linked to physiological needs: these are their hungers, their appetites. Self-conscious beings also have a sense of lack. They have hungers, too, some of which are ultimately grounded in physiological need; they are, however, as we have discussed, dramatically transformed in human beings. What is more, much of the transformation is directed towards sustaining hungers themselves so that the journey towards satisfaction might be prolonged or sustained. This is because there is something unsatisfactory about satisfaction itself. We have examined one aspect of this: for the self-conscious human animal, appetites take the form of propositional attitudes and they are to an increasing extent *narrated*. The state of affairs that satisfies a propositional attitude such as a desire is only one possible instance of what has been generally envisaged. The satisfaction of desire therefore leaves something unsatisfied. Desire regrets its own passing; desire desires itself. What does it really want? It wants not merely some particular object: it wants something that is equal to the desiring self. As Hegel puts it, a self-consciousness can only be gratified by another self-consciousness. At the root of all my desires is a felt lack that can be filled only by being *acknowledged* by another.

At the heart of Hegel's vision are some quite straightforward intuitions, although the book in which he set them out, *Phenomenology of Spirit* ([1807] 1977), is to most of those who have attempted to read it, including the present author, entirely opaque for long stretches. I can become aware of myself only by contrast with something that is *not* myself: *Omnis determination est negatio* – all determination is through negation. It is not sufficient that that Other in virtue of which I am conscious of myself should be a material object. It has no gaze and is not my equal. To be self-conscious requires that I should be conscious of myself as I am in the eyes of one who is conscious of me and who is in some sense my equal: at the very least is self-aware, a self. But things are not as simple, or as benign, as this, for many reason. The most important reason is that in the world as it is so ordered, the relationships between people are rarely between equals and acknowledgement may not be reciprocated. Even where there is no explicit hierarchy of lord and commoner, there are still those who are more needy than others, who have more prestige than others, who are more attractive than others. Historically, the inequalities have been even more stark: there are those who are masters and those who are slaves. Not even the master is well served by this situation.

Let us suppose he demands recognition for what he is in himself – or what he feels himself to be – without acknowledging the slave in turn, whom he cannot accept as his equal and from whom he withholds recognition. It is evident that he is dependent on the slave for this prop to his self-esteem but he does not see this prop as being worthy of him. Nor can he allow that he should be. The unsatisfactory situation of the master is rather like that of the king who requires subservient courtiers whom he despises to stroke his *amour propre* by laughing dutifully at his jokes, praising his skill as a composer, flattering his wisdom. At a deeper level, if to desire someone is to want to possess them, to assimilate them to one's self, this desire is self-defeating; for we cannot possess someone without in some sense destroying them. By abolishing the otherness of the other, desire both possesses and loses its object. We are almost back to the primordial mode of possession: eating, where consumption is destruction.

Hegel regarded this unsatisfactory scenario as potentially remediable. He looked forward to a time when the passionate desire for recognition – which had made much of history a fight to the death for the acquisition of universal prestige and unbounded power – would be satisfied: history would come to a peaceful end in the recognition of all by all. F. H. Bradley, a late-nineteenth-century English philosopher who was greatly influenced by Hegel (but not, fortunately, by his prose style) saw this as a distinct possibility because individuals gain their identity only through communities:

> The child ... is born into a living world ... He does not even think of his own separate self; he grows with his world, his mind fills and orders itself; and when he can separate himself from that world, and know himself apart from it, by that time his self, the object of his self-consciousness, is penetrated, infected, characterised by the existence of others. Its content implies in every fibre relations of community.
>
> (Bradley [1876] 1972: 171–2)

Hegel envisaged a rationally ordered society in which each would acknowledge his essential oneness with the others and desires would be rational in as much as they would promote the common good. They would be an expression of true freedom, unlike the randomly chosen desires of those who imagined they were free because they were able to express their individual wishes.

Sartre, whose commitment to a certain idea of authenticity obliged him to look on the dark side of life, was, more than he was prepared to admit, very taken by Hegel's scenario (and inspired by his abominable prose style). In his first major work *Being and Nothingness* (1957), however, he discounted the possibility of this happy ending. Like Hegel, he placed self-consciousness (he called it the *for-itself*) at the heart of human being and the need for each self-conscious being to find satisfaction in another self-consciousness.

This was especially urgent and inescapable because my awareness of being myself, and my awareness of what I am, are significantly constituted through the gaze of others: I *am* as the Other sees me. Even so, "conflict is the original meaning of being-for-others" and it has no resolution: "While I attempt to free myself from the hold of the Other, the Other is trying to free himself from mine; while I seek to enslave the Other, the Other seeks to enslave me" (Sartre 1957: 364). As if this is not bad enough, neither party can claim victory for the reasons that Hegel foresaw. The conquest, possession, of another which seems to secure my full recognition, fails at the very moment of conquest. If I reduce the Other to an object so that he cannot enslave me with his consciousness, so that he cannot make me an object in his world, his essence as a subject escapes me.

Sartre adds a particularly vicious twist to this in the case of love, the supreme expression of the hunger for others. To love is to wish to be loved by the person one loves. Nothing short of absolute unconditional love will suffice. But once this is secured, the loved one will have lost her freedom: she will be enslaved by her need for love. She will have lost that which made her loveable; for we love that most which is most free and we love in others that which seems to constitute their freedom, among which is their unattainability. What is more, her unconditional love will settle for nothing less than unconditional love in return. So the loved one will be most demanding of love at the time when she is least able to command it: "The lover does not desire to possess the beloved as one possesses a thing. He demands a special sort of appropriation. He wants to possess a freedom as a freedom ... but demands that this freedom should no longer be free" (*ibid.*: 367).

For the early Sartre who wrote *Being and Nothingness*, in which this dismal scenario is set out, there is no happy release from the miserable dialectics of sexual love. (In his later, even worse written, *Critique of Dialectical Reason*, he allowed for cooperation in shared projects. Ordinary life dilutes the metaphysical *slugfest*.) Indeed, it drives lovers to relationships that are usually classified as pathological but which Sartre regards as simply acting out the logic of desire. In sado-masochistic relationships, for example, one or other partner is reduced by pain and/or voluntary bondage and/or degradation to the flesh of which they are made; or, at the very least, to the situation in which their lover imprisons them. By this means, they are rendered almost tangible and their freedom literally graspable, even as it is abjured. The terminus of such activity is death when the impossibility of the lovers' project is revealed for what it is. The corpse, after all, hardly offers the acknowledgement that the self-consciousness sought so frenziedly and its freedom has most definitely come to an end. The incomprehensible horrors that we spoke of at the beginning of this chapter, such as those tolerated by "women who love too much", start to make sense in light of the vision of the conflict between individuals who look to each other for the love they cannot wholeheartedly grant each other. Individuals whose early life, deprived of love, has left them nakedly needy live out the Hegelian metaphysics without dilution or insulation when they fall in with someone who is capable of manipulating their affections.

Sex and the hunger for others

Even if one does not accept Sartre's pessimistic gloss on Hegel, there is something about the sexual expression of the hunger for others that seems doomed to end in dissatisfaction or unhappiness. The intrinsic insatiability of desires that we examined earlier may explain why, for so many (or those at least who are attractive and not constrained by moral qualms), life is marked by an endless quest for new lovers, with the unlimited possibility of novelty and the joy of surprise, uncertainty and relief or gratification at being accepted. Promiscuity, however, does not bring satisfaction either, not anyway at the level at which it is sought. Yes, satiety and exhaustion are supplemented by the satisfaction that comes from arousing the envy of others. But these do not dig down to the metaphysical depths plumbed by the hunger for others that sexual desire intuits, and the longing it awakens. There is always the danger, particularly in those in whom the biological input to sexual desire is more generous, that desire will regress to mere appetite and the hunger for another will shrink to the pursuit of pleasure. This pleasure can become commodified, thus consolidating the regression to appetite. Sexual activity can be reduced to tradable favours, with a bill of fare and a tariff to go with it. The sex trade – which caters for those who are unattractive – is a multi-billion pound industry. The virtual sex of pornography is, according to the feminist lawyer Catherine MacKinnon, now so universal as almost to define contemporary society. Prostitution, even leaving aside the violence, degradation and diseases to which it exposes the providers of services, is undesirable because it takes the separation of sexual appetite from the hunger for others to the limit. A recent study investigating instances of prostitutes who have mysteriously failed to become HIV positive while their fellow workers are dying of AIDS shows just how far this can go. A Kenyan prostitute who has had 50,000 clients (at 37p a time) illustrates the extent to which sexual desire can be reduced to an appetite that in turn reduces its object to a human *pissoir*. Studies in the 1980s, when AIDS first became a matter of concern, documented the frantic sexual activity of certain gay communities in which an individual might have as many as fifty partners over a weekend. The urgency does not diminish with time; indeed, sex addicts find (so they tell us) that sex or the possibility of it dominates virtually every moment of waking life. The insatiability of the sex addict is not simply for the experience of carnal pleasures. After all, his obsession does not drive him to have sex a few thousand times with the same women, but to have sex a few times with a thousand women, irrespective of the cost to them in unhappiness and, even, if he has a conscience, to himself. He is after more than physical sensations.

The reason for this is that sex is never quite reducible to an appetite. The most stupid thing that is said about the sexual act is that it is the most overrated ten seconds in the world. This overlooks the fact that it has huge symbolic significance, even where lovemaking is reduced to rutting and rutting is carried out with remarkable despatch. The most casual sex is woven in with narrative before, during and after the climactic events, although much of the narrative is in the separate heads of the participants rather than shared. In an extreme case, the narrative is truncated to the minimum necessary for a transaction: a brief intersection of personal histories in a moment of impersonal intercourse, as when a drunken squaddie ruts with a prostitute doing tricks to support a drug habit out of control. There is a moment of fantasy enjoyed by the consumer of the sexual pleasure that he is being acknowledged by a self-consciousness, that he is being accepted in a profound sense. This is possible because of the overlap between what is happening between the prostitute and the client and what happens when two people who love each other make love. Unfortunately, while access to the body can be bought, the *person* is not for sale: the fantasy of possessing the person through a body made commercially available is revealed as soon as the transaction is complete. This is why men who seek acknowledgement through commercial sex not infrequently turn violent: they feel frustrated with a women for whom they are only one of a series of clients. They want to be the "special one"; and if they cannot be the special one, they must bring the series to an end.

The hunger for others, in which the longing to be acknowledged and the appetite-fuelled fantasy of possession or of being possessed, and the desire for power or domination, are woven or knotted together in a manner that even the hungry one could not unpick, may take over the individual's life. Where it takes the path of transgression, individuals will risk their happiness, their reputation, the happiness of others, and even their lives. In general, however, our hungers for others are neither pathologized, through frustration, towards violence and abuse, or dissipated in the simulacra provided by the sex industry (where ever more realistic pornography erodes the boundaries between imaginary relationships that are entirely fantasy and real relationships that are largely fantasy). We do not suffer the seemingly contradictory metaphysics of the hunger for others in such a direct or stark way. This is because our lives are already caught up in a multiplicity of activities related to work and leisure and the many intermediate steps each activity involves. Those who embark on relationships that seem to speak to their Hegelian hunger do so from within a complex life, which includes a multitude of relationships to others of different kinds. The self-consciousness that seeks satisfaction in another self-consciousness is already busily engaged in paying gas bills, planning holidays, discharging professional duties and enjoying, or dealing with, ongoing relationships with parents, siblings, children, colleagues, mates and acquaintances. Importantly, there are forms of love – parental love, for example – that have at the heart the desire to give, rather than to receive, love; and there are forms of love that are filled with an affection that is remote from the protopathic hunger for domination and possession that characterizes the Sartrean world where "Hell is other people". And many who are denied ordinary love find compensations – in the acquisition of material power over others, in an absorbing career, in stamp collecting – for being frustrated in their hunger for others. And the most intense hungers may be the foundation of a relationship that will itself be assimilated into a life that is made together out of the intersection of two already complicated lives. Out of this life made together arise the subtle happiness and unhappiness, the joys and sorrows and quiet contentment, of a caring relationship, and a companionship, expressed through a lattice of arrangements, shared responsibility, organization, work, plans, a thousand "unremembered acts of kindness and of love" and dreams. The satisfaction of a fundamental human hunger is replaced by a satisfactory life unfolding and elaborated without seeming limit, with its own unique logic, "until death do us part".

Such a life, however, may be haunted by a lost passion, in the sense of a life lost in living: in duties, in the small satisfactions of a worthwhile existence, in arranging arrangements and being faithful to one's undertakings. There is, after all, something in desire that, above all, desires itself, desires its own intensity, its drama, its simplicity, its clear lines. That there is no true satisfaction of a desire which, being a propositional attitude, is intrinsically general, and does not want to settle for a single, accidental realization of itself, is small comfort. Nevertheless, we may better tolerate our state of active dissatisfaction of frustrated desire or the passive dissatisfaction from loss of desire better through being dissipated into a multitude of secondary preoccupations and projects. Although W. B. Yeats, tormented by unrequited love for Maud Gonne, said that he "hid his face amid a crowd of stars", he might have had to do the same if his suit had been successful. In *Ash Wednesday*, T. S. Eliot spoke of the: "... torment / Of love unsatisfied / The greater torment / Of love satisfied" (Eliot 1954). To avoid "the greater torment of love satisfied" we may reject satisfaction altogether. Barthes tells the following story:

A mandarin fell in love with a courtesan. "I shall be yours" she told him, "when you have spent a hundred nights waiting for me, sitting on a stool, in my garden, beneath my window". But on the ninety-ninth night, the mandarin stood up, put his stool under his arm, and went away.   (1978: 40)

This infinitely suggestive tale has many possible interpretations, the most obvious being power play. To keep another waiting,

Barthes tells us, "is the ancient prerogative of power". The mandarin who walks away says, "Now it is *my* turn to keep *you* waiting". But perhaps the story is really reminding us that it may be better to leave one's desire and its object intact. Even so, there are those who, after the agony of love with all its burden of jealousy, its scalding disappointments, its dry excitements, its intense joy and sorrow, feel that when they were in love was the only time they were truly alive – when *Homo metaphysicalis* lived to the full his contradictory hungers.

Concluding thoughts

If animals have appetites, they do not have them in the way human beings do; and they certainly do not have desires. Desires are uniquely human hungers, for their objects are not entities in the material world but general possibilities in a human world that is constructed out of the pooling of the space of possibility each of us entertains as extending beyond what surrounds us. And it is our fellow human beings who can in various ways awaken our most gnawing human hungers. The supreme object of desire is another creature like ourselves: a desiring self-consciousness. In this respect, Hegel was right: only another self-consciousness can present the promise of satisfaction to a self-consciousness. Where, perhaps, he erred was in his diagnosis of the failure of that promise to materialize. He argued, as we have seen, that in its purest form the hunger for others wants to extract from its object an acknowledgement that is not reciprocated: it wants to *subjugate* its object. This is unsatisfying because the subjugated Other then becomes an unworthy source for the acknowledgement we seek. If, as Spinoza said, we love that most that we see is most free, by binding the other to us in a state of abjection, we extinguish that which we love in the loved one.

The failure of our hunger for others to come to a satisfactory conclusion, I have argued, has less to do with the particular dynamics of love than with the nature of desire itself. Many thinkers have connected the intrinsic insatiability of desire with the nature of our being. For writers as remote from each other as Jacques Lacan and Sartre, the sense of lack that is desire is rooted in the very being of the *self* – that is a lack in Being. I have approached this from another direction by observing that the object of desire is intuited or entertained as a general possibility; any realization of that possibility will be only one possible realization out of an indefinite range. The intuited lack that Lacan and Sartre refer to – in Sartre's case the "worm of nothingness" that "lies coiled in the heart of Being" – would be possible only for a being that had a sense of a world beyond its experiences.

In sexual desire, the choice of one individual to represent the Other can seem arbitrary: the lifelong commitment of marriage is a conscious decision to confer necessity on a contingent choice, a paradox of which more individuals in societies dominated by contract rather than covenant seem more aware and fewer seem prepared to live out or with. The illusion of possessing the entire world of others through one Other – so that one woman is Woman and one man is Man and each is Humankind – is ever more vulnerable as the space of possibility for all of us, in a society in which we are ever further from basic need, expands without limit.

The results are everywhere apparent. Sexual desire can regress to appetite and others lives or their bodies may become consumer items. For men and, increasingly, for woman the sexualized body of the Other is seen as the supreme sweetmeat, eye candy, a tasty morsel. Manuals instruct us on how to enjoy "gourmet" sex. Deeply intimate acts pass between individuals whose relation to one another is otherwise quite distant. This passage from personal desire to impersonal appetite is underwritten by the ubiquity of pornography, where the actions that have been transformed in human beings into the supreme expression of desire are expropriated for – or returned to – the expression of appetite; where desires themselves are simply "needs" that are "catered for"; and sexual intercourse is reduced from an interaction between persons to one between bodies. At the very least, sexuality becomes a scene where a frenzied consumer consumes another who may be either frenzied or salaried.

We are back with the cycle of appetite and satiety; of hunger and hunger for hunger. This is the place where repetition reigns. It is the "Dominion of And". And it is here that we encounter a different kind of hunger; what might be termed a fourth or spiritual hunger, that longs for something that neither an existence given over to the pleasures of consumption nor even the satisfactions of a decent, conscientious, scrupulous, dutiful, life can provide. This is a hunger that builds on awareness of the essentially tragic nature of the other hungers.

4. The fourth hunger

After experience had taught me that all things which frequently take place in ordinary life are vain and futile; when I saw that all the things I feared and which feared me had nothing good or bad save in so far as the mind was affected by them, I determined at last to inquire whether there might be anything which might be truly good and able to communicate its goodness, and by which the mind might be affected to the exclusion of all other things; I determined, I say, to inquire whether I might discover and acquire the faculty of enjoying throughout eternity continual supreme happiness.

(Spinoza 1910: 227)

The hunger of the knowing animal

There is perhaps no more poignant, measured and magisterial statement of the ultimate goal of the contemplative life than these opening lines from Spinoza's *Treatise on the Correction of the Understanding*. "Continual supreme happiness": could there be a better expression of the profoundest hope of humankind, once basic necessities have been met? I have entitled this chapter "The Fourth Hunger", but it could (almost) as well have been called "Spiritual Hunger": a catch-all term for a hunger that still remains when other hungers have been met; when our biological hungers have been addressed; when the hunger for pleasure has passed into a state of sufficiently complex diversity as to be able to keep itself at a distance from the hunger for hunger that is boredom; and when our various forms of our hunger for others – for love, for esteem, for power – have become sufficiently diffused as no longer to have to face their tragic insatiability. A sense of lack, of want, a feeling of unmet need, a hunger still remains. We sense that there is something beyond the pursuit of pleasure, of ever more diverse recreations, and the frustrations of a hunger for others.

John Stuart Mill, who had been brought up in a creed of fundamentalist utilitarianism by his father, eventually acknowledged that he could not subscribe to Bentham's simplistic approach to happiness. For Bentham's "felicific calculus" and the goal of the greatest happiness of the greatest number, it mattered not whether the pleasure on which happiness was founded came from "playing pushpin" or "reading poetry". Mill came to doubt whether there could be a single benchmark for judging activities as desirable and for quantifying pleasure. He proposed a distinction between "higher pleasures" such as those of "the intellect, the feelings and imagination, and of moral sentiments" and "lower pleasures", which involved "mere sensation" or the satisfaction of "animal appetites". Some higher pleasures – particularly intellectual pleasures – might actually be associated with "a certain amount of discontent". Even this adjustment of the crude utilitarianism that he had been force-fed since early childhood did not entirely satisfy him, as we shall see presently.

When our appetites reach into a space of possibility governed by propositional awareness, and are transformed into desires, they are by definition insatiable. This, as we have seen, is most obvious in the case of sexual desires and the hunger for others of which it is the most direct expression. This hunger can be managed only at the cost of losing its intensity or regressing to a hunger for pleasure, and the return to the cycle of endlessly returning appetite followed by satiety. For the most part, in everyday life, the unfiltered desire for possession of, or domination over, others is lost in a complex world where, for the most part, people work together to support a multitude of intermediate ends. The bitter pill of settling for less is sweetened by habits of consumption and pastimes and evolving stories of our lives. Nevertheless, our awareness of our pacified hungers – of hungers suppressed, thwarted or fobbed off – remains.

The failure of one's life to reach a climax at which all hungers are satisfied without that satisfaction ushering in anticlimax may awaken a sense of mere succession, of repetition, of a lack of adding up. In Georg Büchner's great play *Danton's Death*, the eponymous hero, the first president of the dreaded Committee of Public Safety after the French Revolution, expresses this crushing sense of the monotony of existence, of the long littleness of a life composed of a thousand projects with their million component steps:

> It's very wearisome every day first to drag on one's shirt and then one's breeches; and to crawl every night into a bed, and every morning out of it. And to set one's foot always in front of the other. And who can suggest a better way?
>
> It's a sad thought. And that millions have done it already – that millions will do it all over again   (Büchner 1952: 148)

Human life can seem to break down into endlessly iterated large and small cycles. As for the one who lives that life, he or she seems like a Humean being, one who is, rather than has, a succession of experiences. There is a feeling of shallowness, of diffusion, of weightlessness. Nothing, beyond the means to survival and threats to comfort and to safety, seems serious. Philip Larkin describes how, even in an era when religion is in retreat, we will still gravitate to holy ground: "Since someone will forever be surprising / A hunger in himself to be more serious" ("Church Going", in Larkin 1988). This hunger, a response to an "unbearable lightness of being", is awoken not only by the sense of being caught up in a non-additive succession of experiences but by two other features of our conscious, indeed self-conscious life.

The first is knowledge of our finitude: that we are only a small part of the world we know; and, as a correlative of this, that we shall not live forever. While everything in this restless universe is transient, only one kind of object in it is explicitly aware of this giant fact: the human animal. In this sense, Yeats's seemingly paradoxical assertion that "Man has invented death" is true. Even satiety and comfort are edged with intimations of death, the source of that fear of sitting still that Pascal identified as lying at the root of so many of ills. "If man were happy, the less he were diverted the happier he would be". However, he knows, sometimes remembers, and occasionally fully realizes his condition:

> Imagine a number of men in chains, all under sentence of death, some of whom are butchered each day in the sight of others; those remaining see their own condition in that of their fellows, and looking at each other with grief and despair await their turn. This is an image of the human condition.
>
> (Pascal 1995: 137)

We know that "the last act is bloody, however fine the rest of the play. They throw earth over your head and it is finished for ever" (*ibid.*: 53). All of this may make our hungers more intense, or more urgent; or our pleasures may be poisoned by the knowledge that the ultimate end of all our purposes is purposelessness; that our strivings are in vain. Our pleasures will vanish and those things that we build *en route* to our pleasures or as consolation for elusive satisfactions will also vanish.

The second is the very nature of our consciousness, of which knowledge is only the most developed and distinctive part. As noted in Chapter 3, we live in a world of material objects that we experience as surrounding, but separate from, us; and this encircling world is itself a small island in a huge ocean, located in a much larger world of facts. The world we occupy is cast adrift in a world we know, which is itself cast adrift in a world we merely know of. This widest world is a great echoing space – a space of rumours in which we are lost – into which we reach with our expectations, anticipations, images and ideas, and, words, words, words, variously charged with emotions of duty, love, hope, fear, joy, and terror. Given over to this world, we feel that we are, as Franz Kafka said in a letter, "separated from everything by a hollow space" (quoted in Heller 1961: 175).

All of this amounts to a new kind of emptiness and a correlative hunger. This emptiness is more important as life is ever more complexly mediated and our essence is attenuating to e-sense. The challenge to be "fully there", here and now, is more pressing as we collude in being torn apart by distractions. Unfortunately, the commonest response to this, the fourth hunger, is to try to feed it with nourishment appropriate to the first three. We eat more, we pursue pleasure and distraction more frantically, we consume more avidly, we are ever more obsessed with prestige, with the various forms of acknowledgement we want from others. The increasingly discarnate nature of our lives may in part account for the obsession with ever more frenzied carnality. Predictably, we remain dissatisfied.

We may characterize this fourth hunger in different ways, capturing different aspects of it. We may see it as being driven by the prospect of "enjoying throughout eternity continual supreme happiness". Or as a longing for a mode of repleteness that is not a state of boredom but of fullness of being. Or as the desire to round off, by gathering up, and putting together, the sense of one's life and one's self, perhaps in the further hope of finding a permanent significance that goes beyond the ebb and flow of daily life. Or as a longing for a wholeness that replicates at the level of self-consciousness or one's life the unity of one's body and its organic being. At the heart of the fourth hunger is a hunger for meaning, for more consciousness and of a different kind. In what follows I shall touch on different ways of trying to achieve that in order to round off the sense of the world.

A higher purpose

For many, the fourth hunger is satisfied, or pre-empted, by dedication to a higher human purpose. The mission to make the world a better place must surely be one of the most benign manifestations of the sense of inner lack. Righting wrongs, alleviating the misfortunes of the unfortunate, finding new ways of preventing or dealing with the hazards arising from the natural world, assisting the needy: all of these may form the basis of a lifetime that is both satisfying and worthy. Such a life does speak to many aspects of the fourth hunger, as well as providing much incidental satisfaction of other hungers, in particular the need to be admired, esteemed or acknowledged. A "great project" seems to have its significance guaranteed and built into it. What is more, since it extends over a long time, it binds our days together: life has a form, is informed with an evolving story, and the self is stitched internally. The hungers for more seriousness and for more coherence are addressed. Those for whom the fourth hunger has taken this form have, for the most part, made this world a better place.

For some there is a special joy in self-denial, in putting others' needs ahead of one's own, comparable to the joy of fasting. Archbishop Tillotson's claim that "There is no sensual pleasure in the world comparable to the delight a good man takes in doing good" seems momentarily plausible, notwithstanding the slightly suspicious source, which may suggest a confusion between the pleasure of doing good for its own sake and the pleasure of exhibiting one's self as a good person. Shortly before his death, Bentham sent a letter to a friend's young daughter, which contained this deeply moving passage:

> Create all the happiness you are able to create: remove all the misery you are able to remove. Every day will allow you to add something to the pleasure of others, or to diminish some of their pains. And for every grain of enjoyment you sow in the bosom of another, you shall find a harvest in your own bosom; while very sorrow which you pick out from the thoughts and feelings of a fellow creature shall be replaced by beautiful peace and joy in the sanctuary of your soul.
>
> (Quoted in Layard 2005: 235–6)

It is not so easy to shed one's appetite for one's appetites. The fact that the pleasure of doing good is not pursued as vigorously as the sensual pleasures supposedly less intense, and the joy of dedication to a higher purpose seems less attractive to most people than the joy of sex, or of being a dedicated follower of a particular football team, may be because much doing good consists of rather humdrum activities. Even great projects break down to small components, a myriad of intermediate steps and interim ends. The big picture, which stitches the self together and carries the larger significance, is lost. Indeed, the satisfaction of achievement often proves rather illusory. The higher purpose, the great project to which one has dedicated one's self, hides behind the small aims, the minute interim goals, through which they are expressed or achieved. It is very difficult to keep one's larger sense alive in the logistical jungle, and the multiple frustrations and the petty details of everyday goodness. From the point of view of hungering human beings, goodness is not good enough.

The most poignant example of the insufficiency of doing good is described in Mill's *Autobiography*. Brought up from his earliest childhood to a life dedicated to improving the lot of his fellows, this wonderfully generous-spirited, thoughtful, talented man found himself assailed by doubts in his early twenties. A great depression descended on him:

> In this frame of mind it occurred to me to put the question directly to myself: "Suppose that all your objects in life were realized; that all the changes in institutions and opinions which you are looking forward to could be completely effected at this very instant: would this be a great joy and happiness to you?" And an irrepressible self-consciousness distinctly answered, "No!". At this my heart sank within me: the whole foundation on which my life was constructed fell down. All my happiness was to have been found in the continual pursuit of this end. The end had ceased to charm, and how could there ever again be any interest in the means? I seemed to have nothing left to live for. (Mill 1989: 112)

Mill found his salvation in art; in particular the poetry of William Wordsworth.

Art

Schopenhauer claimed that art was valued because it released us from the endless treadmill of the will: of proliferating hungers whose satiation brought only boredom or, out of the hunger for hunger, yet more hungers. By means of art, he said, we are liberated from ourselves in disinterested contemplation: "we celebrate the Sabbath of the penal servitude of willing" (Schopenhauer 1969: I, 196).Others, most notably Nietzsche, have adopted the opposite view: that art as its apex celebrates the will to power, especially as expressed in striving for greatness. It elevates hunger, rather than unchains us from it. Perhaps there is partial truth in both views.

Could it be that art enables us so completely and perfectly to experience our experiences that they truly satisfy us and our hunger may be abated for a while without boredom and emptiness taking its place? Let us examine how this might be.

Ours is a curious condition. The consciousness and self-consciousness with which we are burdened place us in the situation of being creatures that have woken to a greater or lesser extent out of the state of an organism to an understanding of sorts of our own nature and the great world in which we are located. Half-awakened, we are constantly engaged in making explicit sense of the world and, most importantly, of our fellow human beings. This sense remains tantalizingly incomplete and stubbornly local. With it comes the feeling that we have not fully realized our own existence, not fully realized that we exist, not fully realized the scale and scope of what we are and of the world we live in. It is a kind of existential numbness that we feel with an especial intensity when our pleasures fail to match our expectations. When experiences are sought for their own sake, we have noted, we seem unable to experience them adequately: meals, pastimes, looked-forward to meetings, love affairs seem to pass through us – as we pass through them – without any sides being touched. The most common response to this is to seek out more, and more varied and more complex, experiences: in short, to increase the level and intensity of experience. As the pace of consumption quickens, as we move from one thing to another, in increasing haste, we become aware of something else: our experiences seem insufficiently connected – they do not add up. We may characterize this lack of connectedness in different ways: that we are always small-sampling our lives and our worlds; that we have no overview on ourselves; that we are condemned to live in the "Dominion of And" or the "Kingdom of And Then, And Then", in which we pass on from one thing to another, without ever being fully at any of them. It seems as if we are fated to die *without ever having fully grasped our being there*. In part, this is because we cannot close the gap between what we experience ourselves at any moment as being and what we know; between our ideas and our experiences, our experiences and the life and world of which they are a part. We cannot, in short, heal the wound of "de-experience" that knowledge opens up in the world of experience.

Consider the most sustained attempt to dwell in the Kingdom of Ends that most of us undertake: the annual summer holiday when we are liberated for a uniquely long period of time from the productive process in order to seek experience for its own sake. The difficulties that attend this secular *haj* tell us a lot about human consciousness and why it needs art. The top and bottom of it is that we cannot fully holiday: there is no action or experience corresponding purely to the verb "to holiday". If we drown ourselves in the experiences of the moment we lose sight of the holiday that we sought; and if we try to keep the overall idea of the holiday in view, we lose the immediacy and completeness of experience. This is a large-scale expression of the fact that propositional attitudes cannot be satisfied because they are cast in general form and any given realization is too particular. That is why we seem all the time to be either *en route* to the holiday or to be drifting away from it, losing it in distractions. We can never really arrive on holiday because we journey towards *ideas* of experience that no experience can realize. (Recall Flaubert: "Wine has a taste unknown to those who drink it. It lies in the idea alone.") That is why the moment of arrival seems to elude us – and systematically. Journeys end only in more journeys, constituting the activity one had arrived at or for, taking one past the point of arrival. And so it goes, until it is time for departure and the journeys that lead all the way home and back to the Kingdom of Means.

The ideas of experience, that haunt actual experiences and find them wanting, are derived either from anticipation shaped by words and pictures or, when it is a case of re-visiting, from those postcards of the mind that have developed in our memory. Ideas differ from any possible experience in two rather fundamental ways: first, sense experience is baggy, obese with contingencies (my conception of the cliff walk or the two-hour surf in the sea did not include any of the very particular items of which it is composed – that particular missed wave, that seagull flying overhead, that shower of rain); and, secondly, the idea is given all at once in an instant of anticipation or recall, while the experience unfolds over time. The idea has a clear form that the experience lacks. Experience is thus riddled by a sense of insufficiency: we feel that we are not quite experiencing it. Hence the difficulty of arrival.

Why experience sought for its own sake is undermined by the general ideas it fails fully to instantiate goes to the heart of the peculiar condition of the human animal, of the propositional awareness that constitutes so much of human consciousness, and which we discussed in the previous chapter. The idea is cast in a general form, referring as it is does to the space of possibility, that no sensory experience can realize, or "saturate". Because we are creatures who are aware "*That x* is, or is not, or might be, the case", we are not dissolved into our experiences; on the contrary, we are located in a world that surrounds us with ever-increasing circles of multi-layered general possibilities. We try to live with our senses a life that is always looking beyond our senses. That is why we are haunted by a sense of not being quite there; of not being able fully to experience our experiences in a way that connects with our wider self, our wider world, our life as a whole.

Art, I believe, addresses this hunger for wholeness of experience and connectedness between experiences. It does, of course, bring us pleasures not greatly different from the hedonistic pleasures we discussed in Chapter 2. And the creation of art, or simply becoming an art connoisseur, has a complex social dimension that plays into the hunger for others and the search for self-esteem. What we are interested in here, though, is in its capacity to address the fourth hunger. Two characteristics of art, corresponding to the two concerns I have highlighted, are most directly relevant to dealing with our half-awakened, divided state: form and connectedness. Let me discuss form first.

We may interpret the mismatch between experience and the idea of it – as a result of which we somehow do not experience our experiences – as a disconnection between content and form. The content is the actual experience, with all the sense data served up by the accidents of the moment; and the form is the idea of experience. In a truly realized work of art, in contrast with our lives, form and content are in harmony, like the *recto* and *verso* of a single sheet of paper. This is most easily illustrated by music, which, for the present discussion, we may think of as the paradigm art. (As Walter Pater famously said, "all art constantly aspires towards the condition of music".) Think of the relationship between sound and idea – or form – in the experience of a melody. Each note is fully present as a physical event and yet is manifestly part of a larger whole, of an idea. There is no conflict between the form or idea of the music and its actual instants. Our moments of listening are imbued with a sense of what is to come and what has passed. The form to which the music conforms – that ties what has gone and what is to come with each other and with what is present – shines through its individual moments. There is both movement and stasis; in Aristotelian terms, the unfolding sound realizes form as "the unmoving moved".

Admittedly, the music has its journeys – it manifestly is a journey from a beginning to an end – and in great music we feel as if we have travelled great distances to and through a remote soundscape. But the journeying is never merely a piece of *en route*: the unfolding of the form fills and fulfils the sensation of the present moment with the past and the future, rather than undermining it with the past and the future. The leitmotif, recurring throughout the music like an involuntary memory, ties together the beginning, the middle and the end, making it all one. The retrospective light it casts on all that has gone before creates the feeling that we have been arriving all the time and that, indeed, we are arrived. Which is why there are moments when, listening to great music, we have the sense of enjoying our own consciousness – its present and its past – in italics.

For Schopenhauer, music was the supreme art because it was a direct expression of the will, which was the inner nature of the world. The musical journey away from and back to the home key, its restless peregrinations through sounds from silence back to silence, articulates in the purest, least mediated, way the striving of the will. Even if one does not fully accept this extraordinarily beautiful idea, it is possible to see in music a perfected representation of the cycle of appetite and satiety, liberating us from both. And a *perfection* of emotion and of desire. When Felix Mendelssohn said that "the thoughts expressed to me by music are not too indefinite to be put into words, but, on the contrary, too definite", he was hinting at how music might reconcile the generality of the space of possibility and the particularity of sensory experience; how desire, which is intrinsically general, may indeed find actual satisfaction.

So much for form and experiencing our experiences. What of the connectedness of experiences and their integration into a greater whole? Connectedness across occasions – so that any moment reaches into a wider world than is available to it in ordinary life – is best illustrated by what is achieved in narrative fiction. In practice, we are always trying to redeem our sense of being fragmented by means of the stories we recount about ourselves and each other and our world. In most stories we tell we aim to put ourselves in a good light, but more important than that we try to put ourselves in any kind of light, to give ourselves sharp edges, thus dimly reflecting our hunger to make things hang together and have a clearer outline than in the fuzzy muddle of real-time experience. This is greatly elaborated in fiction in that extraordinary device called the plot. Both great literature and ephemeral garbage use plots to tie together persons, places, things and themes by means of extended and interconnected stories. Literature, however, realizes – makes real and present – the road the story takes; opens views either side of the road; and connects numerous roads with one another. While trash-fiction draws a blurred line, faded with familiarity, across an otherwise blank canvas, great novels create microcosms that, by reproducing the multidimensional complexity of the macrocosm, make more of the world mind-portable, and so extend "available consciousness" and possibly even our human sympathy, although that is another story.

From its elevated viewpoint, created when so much is brought together within a single cover, our greatly extended view gathers together what we have known, suspected, thought of, imagined, with a consequent mitigation of "And"; a "de-scattering" of our scattered, tatty, messy lives, calling back diffuseness to concentration, through its wider, deeper connectedness. The artist makes connections – at the level of metaphor, form, memory, life, world – in order to be equal in imagination to at least some of what he knows or is known.

Unfortunately, a work of art does not bring our hungers to a satisfactory end; but it does afford a glimpse of a way of seeing, and hence a way of being, in which our consciousness – beyond the first, second and third hungers – progresses towards a kind of perfection beyond the cycle of hunger and satiety. As an exemplar it addresses the wound in consciousness opened up by knowledge, or more generally propositional awareness. It acknowledges, and consoles us for, our customary lack of "thereness" – the result of our being eaten away from within by insatiable or frustrated desires – and lack of connectedness – the result of the endless "And" of our recurrent and proliferating hungers and the satiety that may come in their wake. But a great work of art is a lens as well as a jewel and through it we may continue the processing of widening our consciousness. It invites us to view our own lives with the eyes of an artist. It says: this is how the world might be experienced; now go forth and experience it thus.

In this discussion of art, I have not separated the producer from the consumer. One may assume that they have the same underlying motive: to heal the wound opened up in consciousness by propositional awareness, most clearly evident in the gap between sense experience and factual knowledge. In the case of artists, however, the gap is felt more intensely and, of course, there are circumstances (not the least of these being the happy accident of having a gift) that make them able and willing to devote their lives to creativity. In a small way, the true recipient of art replicates the creative activity of the artist in order to experience the work. In the case of both the artist and the audience, however, there is another problem.

Just as we noted how sexual relations and even sexual love can regress from a human desire to an appetite, satisfied by a pleasure-giving operation whose components may be commodified as in the sex trade, combined with the fantasy of being esteemed, so art, too, which begins as a commodity that is bought and sold, can be claimed for consumption and become a series of consumer items. The "Dominion of And" may return as the appreciative viewer, listener or reader becomes a consumer of a succession of experiences that are no longer elevated above the experiences of daily life. The search for a life more abundant, and more connected, in which the gap between idea and experience is at least temporally healed, can slip into the pursuit of pleasures, in which art takes its place alongside other pastimes and sensual enjoyments. This may take us again to the path of accelerating consumption; because the work of art does not perfect our consciousness but gives us a glimpse of a perfected consciousness, a life devoted to art may simply be one in which one series of "And thens…" is replaced by another: "gourmet food + consumer durables + sexual partners" by "symphonies + poems". In the case of the producer it will be one work of art after another, as the conscience that demands productivity overrides the deeper conscience that asks for the one work that answers to the artist's longing to encompass the world, recreating it in his own image; grasping it as a way of eluding or revoking its grasp.

Religion

The fourth hunger arising out of the very nature of the consciousness of the human animal – propositional, self-conscious, self-divided – can be characterized in different ways: a hunger for experiences that are really experienced; a longing for coherence; a search for more and wider significance; a quest for experiences that reach beyond themselves, even beyond experience, and illuminate one's life more widely; a pursuit of meaning that stretches through one's life or gives one's life the character of a meaningful journey. The reality of the fourth hunger is demonstrated by how much individuals are willing to give up for it; in particular, how it will displace the other hungers.

It is interesting, in view of our overall theme, to think of the many ways in which religion and eating intersect. The sacrifice of food, diverting nutriment from our stomachs to the sky; the prohibitions against eating certain sorts of food, or certain foods on certain days, or certain combinations of foods; and the obligation to fast: while all of these modes of "sanctified eating" may seem to have a practical interpretation, they collectively underline how the denial of nature, through the thwarting of natural appetites, is a way of underlining the supernatural character and answerability of humankind.

This is most starkly expressed in the lives of those saints, holy men and mystics who undertake the supreme ordeal of prolonged fasting. Such a denial of primary hungers signifies commitment to a hunger that transcends the body: a hunger for life beyond the body. It is as if one could communicate with an invisible world by progressing towards invisibility, thinning towards a state where one becomes translucent to eternity and porous to the divine. In some cases, it was not so much the nutritional value of food as the sensual pleasure associated with eating it that was avoided. Clare Gambacorta of Pisa mixed ashes with her scraps of food so that eating them would be an even more unpleasant experience. Catherine of Sienna managed to overcome her residual desire for food by carefully gathering into a ladle the pus from the suppurating, cancerous breast of a lady she was attending and drinking it. (Whether or not she obtained the patient's consent we are not told.) That night she had a visitation from Christ and with this consolation she no longer had need of food nor could her stomach digest it.

The apical intersection between eating and religion is the consumption of the gods, as in the sacrament of the Christian Eucharist, itself derived from previous pagan rituals. It is deeply poignant to think that at the highest level of spiritual aspiration we return to something as closely connected with the basic hunger as oral ingestion. Unfortunately, the participants do not take on the properties of the deity they ingest nor, in all honesty, do they expect to do so. The weight of the quotidian with its cycles of hunger and satiety rules undiminished. Like other acts of consumption, eating the Body and Blood of Christ has to be repeated again and again and again.

Perhaps the profoundest of all the religious myths, the Genesis story, is a startling assertion of the link between hunger and the opening of the wound in self-consciousness. After eating the forbidden fruit, Adam and Eve were self-conscious: their eyes were opened and they saw that they were naked. Henceforth, food would no longer grow of its own accord. Humans would (to echo Engels and Marx) be distinguished from the rest of creation in virtue of having "to produce the means of their subsistence" – by the sweat of their brow. This fall from Paradise was an awakening to, and therefore out of, a world in which we had hitherto been happily at home. It was the beginning of not only the human life of labour but also of de-experiencing and of the self-consciousness (remember the fig leaf) that seeks, and does not find, satisfaction in another self-consciousness. (Eve's quarrel with Adam was portentous.) Since then we have reduced the amount of sweat our brows have to secrete in producing the wherewithal to live – although we endlessly define upwards the wherewithal – but at the price of ever more desolating de-experiencing. The thorny, thistly wastes into which Adam and Eve were expelled may have been made more hospitable but the hunger that awoke with self-consciousness has, if anything, become sharper.

Any treatment of religion, even one as superficial and cursory as what is to follow, however, has to acknowledge that religious observance has a multitude of prompts and triggers, serves a myriad of purposes and is encrusted with many layers of secondary phenomena: the particular form of a sacred dance; detailed dietary and other observances; the endless deliberations of scholars. It is not easy to see what the quintessence of religion is. Removing all of those things that seem accidental may yield the same kind of reward as came to those who, in search of the heart of the artichoke, stripped off all its leaves. At the core of religion is the sense of the sacred and of a hidden reality that transcends daily life. This hidden reality has a huge and incalculable influence on our well-being and through its visible interpreters – the priests – guides us as to our conduct and to our expectations. In some religions the hidden reality may be a power that intercedes on our behalf and, in the case of the relatively recent religions of salvation, inhabits and curates another place where, if we are good or lucky or both, we may ourselves come to enjoy eternal life. Those notions are entangled in this-worldly power relations, in the affirmation of one's allegiance to or membership of a visible group on earth, and in customs and habits that may be to a greater or lesser degree automatic and even uncomprehended. Religion may also serve this-worldly purposes: giving a sense of controlling the unforeseen events or the chronic hard luck that is the lot of most people over history; promoting values that support the status quo and making life bearable at least for some and unbearable for others; and so on. Much of this purpose will have lost its significance with changing times: some functions of prayer and ritual have been superseded by technology, and divine commandments by internalized conscience and the force of law.

For this reason, we have to acknowledge that there is little in religion that speaks directly to the fourth hunger; and where it does, it does so with inescapable adulterants. Those who devote their lives to an unchanging, all-knowing force, sometimes called God, may by this means add significance and coherence to their existence and make the vanity of human experiences of less moment. But in so doing, they have to take into their life a multitude of observances and beliefs and commitments that are remote from the fourth hunger. Arguments over the *filioque* clause, the accidents of the Islamic world picture, the particular order in which an observant Jew puts on his shoes, the form of the obedience a Buddhist monk owes to his superior: these are connected only indirectly or tangentially with the fourth hunger – with the desire for a coherent, life, a self that has true substance, a significance that goes beyond the many daily, weekly and yearly cycles of hunger, need, lack, want and satiety. Indeed, the religious life itself may break down to many activities, aims and their associated hungers that are not qualitatively different from those that occupy the consciousness of unbelievers.

Even so, the idea of God, and a God to whom one's being owes its existence and to whom that existence is addressed, and in which it has its meaning and purpose and from which it takes its true direction, might seem to answer to the fourth hunger. To subordinate one's will to the will of God, to make of one's self and one's life, with its pell-mell of events and actions and preoccupations, its cycles of hunger and satiety, a gift returned to a God that gave it in the first place, would seem to answer to the need for a wholeness, unity, coherence, an existential integrity that goes all the way down and puts all other hungers in their place. Such a way of living is captured in Kierkegaard's notion of a "purity of heart", which is "to will one thing". The one who wills this one thing is an individual, isolated before a God, in unmediated contact with the true, cognate intentional object of his conscience. Unfortunately, such purity of heart requires a life free of distractions, days unburdened by multiplicity, and an access to God that is uncluttered by the Byzantine mediations represented in complex doctrines, elaborate observances and a plethora of actions that have only a distant relationship to the central existential aim: in short, a steady religious commitment that is almost void of all the characteristics of actual religious beliefs and of the acts of devotion that fill the lives of believers. In reality, it is impossible to will one thing through religion: to give one's entire life and self to an entity that lies between an abstract concept, a person and a fire of terror and joy in one's heart, and that unites a moral teacher or lawgiver with the Big Bang.

All of these difficulties apply even if one leaves aside others that are greater and more evident. Most religious doctrines are internally inconsistent; or inconsistent with the experience of the world. Belief requires much suspension of disbelief and it is difficult to do so without suspending more of one's self. Religions are also incompatible with one another. This makes the choice of religion the child of an accident – of birth, culture or experience – precisely in the place where contingency should be transcended. The multiplicity of religions, of course, makes for more than dilemmas in the transcendental shopping mall: it foments division, polarization and conflict, and embeds individuals more deeply in a particular parish of human culture, possibility, identity. Religion should permeate every aspect of one's life – that is the essence of the willing of one thing that answers to the hunger to be more than an endless cycle of local needs, appetites, desires, lacks, wants and their local fulfilments – but the interaction between religion and the multiform surfaces of life tends to be on life's terms rather than that of the invisible world. Churchgoing as a fashion display, bigoted dislike of those who have different beliefs, the exercise of power and petty spite: these, rather than a blazing sense of a self unified in the imagined gaze of God, are the day-to-day reality of religion. It is not for nothing that the word most immediately and strongly associated with "ritual" is "empty".

If religion does speak to the fourth hunger, and offer liberation from the Humean state of being a succession of experiences, of being a conduit for a life one does not somehow fully live, what it has to say is inevitably interwoven with many other things that have nothing to do with the fourth hunger and everything to do with the other three. Most of the religions that are on offer were the products of times in which the human condition was utterly different from that in which we hunger today. Their assumptions, attitudes and purposes fit awkwardly with a contemporary reality in which a universal rationalism is broadcast in the technology that fills the world. The merging of an account of the origin of the universe, the nature of a particular race of people on earth and moral teaching does not resonate in much of the world where physics, a sense of national identity, history with all its accidents, and ethics, other worldly authority and worldly power, tend to belong to different compartments of consciousness.

What is still living about religion, alas, is the individual and collective self-hatred that seems to energise its most passionate adherents – vividly and sometimes rather disgustingly exemplified in self-torturing holy men and women – and the even greater hatred of others who do not share the form of self-hatred that it licenses. And it is not at all clear that, if one removed the many wrappings that enclose religion and serve identity and power politics at a domestic, local and geopolitical level, and the great structures of observance, belief, ritual and institution, there would be much left to feed the hungers of those who feel the fourth hunger; or, indeed, much left at all.

In the Faust lane: science and philosophy

In one of the most famous and moving passages in philosophy, Pascal spoke of man as "a thinking reed":

> Man is but a reed, the weakest in nature; but he is a thinking reed. It does not take the whole Universe in arms to crush him. A vapour, or a drop of water, is enough to kill him. But, if the Universe were to crush him, man would still be nobler than his killer. For he knows that he is dying, and that the Universe has an advantage over him; the Universe knows nothing of this.
>
> Our whole dignity consists, therefore, in thought. By thought we must raise ourselves, and not by space or time which we have no means of filling.   (Pascal 1961: 100)

Our greatness lies in thought: the self-same faculty that reveals us to ourselves as vulnerable, weak, a fiery particle of hunger, pride and ambition, and lost in the "eternal silence of the infinite spaces" that terrified Pascal. It seems, then, as if our salvation may lie in the extension of thought. This does not merely apply to our physical salvation or to some putative salvation in a benign eternity. It is about appeasing a spiritual hunger that we may characterize as "a desire to round off the sense of the world".

Religion, too, offers to complete the sense of the world; better still, it proposes a point where our many hungers, culminating in the hunger for enduring significance, and our very selves converge in the bosom of the deity. There is, however, an important difference: the truths of religion are revealed and are already there. The struggle of the religious knower is to understand, to believe, to embrace, to be equal to, already existing answers. The struggle of the secular seeker begins with questions and truths that have to be painstakingly arrived at by a different kind of cognitive pilgrimage

– a process of enquiry and method that is undertaken collectively by mankind – or by scientists, philosophers and other thinkers on their behalf. The ethos of science and philosophy is to start without assumptions. This is variously seen as being anti-dogmatic, following the argument where it leads, or being true to the facts. This is a little self-flattering: humanity is always starting out from somewhere and its enquiries are encircled by unquestioned frames, implicit assumptions and inherent values and as individuals we get most of our answers off a shelf maintained by the collective. But in the case of science it is true enough to reality to have delivered material well-being beyond the wildest dreams of our ancestors.

Science does not, however, ultimately answer to the hunger for coherent meaning. First, there are many sciences and their catalogue of facts, concepts and laws is endless. Even the facts of our own case are multiple and seem difficult to inhabit, to fill with our being, in order that we might become subjectively the objective thing that we are. At the most fundamental or general level – as we approach a theory of everything – there is a simplicity, but this comes at the price of emptying its discourse of specific content and of lived meaning. The universe as viewed through a handful of equations approximating to a theory of everything is almost without substance: the multicoloured world overflowing with meaning is reduced to a static charcoal outline, to the mathematical form of a mathematical form, void of content. Those who want to appease their hunger for significance by exercising the power of the thinking reed, enclosing the universe that makes them seem insignificant in thought, will find that they are living on "the acorns and grass of knowledge … for the sake of truth". The completion of the scientific world picture in a theory of everything, even if it were possible, would simply be the apotheosis of de-experience. And of course it is not possible: the more we know, the more we are aware of our ignorance. Science, in the end, offers us only provisional and incomplete sense as does everyday life, and, although that sense is magnified, so too is the feeling of its incompleteness. The loose ends are more numerous and longer. We are dwarfed in the world that scientific knowledge reveals to us; and we are dwarfed by that knowledge; and we are dwarfed by the ocean of known unknowns in which what we know floats. No wonder the Nobel Prize-winning astrophysicist Steven Weinberg was moved to observe that "the more the universe seems comprehensible, the more it also seems pointless". His claim needs adjustment: it is when we comprehend the world through the lens of science that it seems meaningless. The image that results is magnificent but emptied of the personal, voided of content corresponding to actual experience, and sometimes (as in the case of quantum theory, the greatest of all scientific monuments) actually incomprehensible.

Philosophy, too, begins from questions, although it does not settle for the multiplicity of physical science. To use Jan Patočka's distinction, philosophy aims at "knowing the whole" while science aims at "knowing all there is". It originates in the desire to transcend the world of thought and experience in order to arrive at a vantage point from which it can be seen as a whole. At its greatest it combines the toughest, most rigorous sense of reality with the most tingling sense of possibility. It opens dormer windows in our consciousness. And its most fundamental aim – to enlarge and clarify our understanding of the world, even to make the world mind-portable – overlaps with that of art. It, too, strives to liberate us, at least at the cognitive level, from the "Dominion of Eternal And". Indeed, it would like to round off the sense of the world. Like art, it fails to achieve this wholly; but philosophy's failure is more profound.

For philosophy, even more than science, tends to X-Ray rather than see the world, looking straight past or straight through it. It connects experiences together by emptying them. While this is the source of its true greatness – and life without philosophical enquiry driven by wonder, joy, terror and awe is distinctly anencephalic – it is also a profound flaw. It is aseptic and lacks the armpit odour of reality. The categories with which philosophy at the highest level deals – Being, Mind, Matter, Consciousness, and so on – are as empty of the concrete particulars of existence as the terms in the most general scientific equations.

When it comes to addressing the fourth hunger, therefore, philosophy may not prove very nutritious. For there is a sense in which the most ambitious, the widest, philosophical thoughts are unthinkable. Even where their content does not forbid their being thought, philosophical thoughts seem resistant to being thought with the requisite completeness. It is easy to see why this is the case. There is, first of all, the huge scope of most philosophical thoughts: they aim at, or pretend to, the widest possible generality. Now we are used to factual thoughts of mind-boggling scope: for example, "The suffering experienced as a result of the Second World War was immense". Indeed, much of the time, when we are dealing with objects of knowledge by description as opposed to those of direct acquaintance (to use Russell's distinction), we feel that our verbal reach exceeds our mental grasp. Things, however, are different with philosophical discourse, partly because its scope is boundless. This cannot, however, be the whole story; after all science talks about "matter", "energy", "the universe" and so on. Philosophy, however, is special in one respect.

As Gabriel Marcel pointed out, the subject matter of philosophy actually encroaches on the philosopher. This is why philosophy is more promising than science as a food for the fourth hunger. If the goal of philosophy, whether it is the philosophy of mind, or of the self, or of being, or substance, is to arrive at a coherent account of the totality of what is there, this will include the philosopher. Unlike science (which is resolutely third-person, or no-person), philosophy, although it attempts to be objective, rational and impersonal, cannot leave out consciousness or the first-person. Which is why when we first philosophize we are often assailed by vertigo, and by the sensation that we are going to spin into a maelstrom of self-consciousness. For much of the time, philosophers, like scientists, deal with problems "out there". Philosophy is specialized and breaks down topics into problems that are addressed piecemeal. But if we are serious, we want ultimately to bring everything together, perhaps in a small cluster of thoughts that can be held in mind and thought. Even though we seem never to arrive at this goal, it remains a "regulative idea" (to use Kant's phrase) and is ultimately what distinguishes philosophy from mere puzzle solving.

We often forget this because philosophy provides us with so many intermediate, provisional satisfactions: following arguments, winning debates, getting to know what X thought and Y said, and seeing how X influenced Y. It is also true that it is possible to entertain philosophical ideas in a way that makes us feel that we are really having them, even when we fall a long way short of fully possessing, or being possessed, by those thoughts. Anyone who is truly seized by the impulse to philosophize knows that it is more than just another mode of cognitive productivity (*pace* professional philosophers who have to produce papers) and the local satisfaction of dealing with brainteasers. Yes, we can argue, or follow, arguments towards philosophical ideas, and argue, or follow, arguments away from them, and cite them and knowingly allude to them, but in doing so we remain only a conduit for them. This is adequate in the case of science, where ideas are subordinated to some other purpose; they are not being thought for their own sake.

What would it be truly to have a philosophical understanding that answered to the fourth hunger for a rounded sense of the world, a conclusive mode of being? I imagine a stream of thought arriving at a destination, coming to a halt and widening into a lagoon that not only has the shape of the idea the philosopher has tried to convey, but also of one's self, thinking it, so that one is given over to it without remainder, as it were. This is impossible, not the least because thoughts are always token thoughts, thoughts that occur at a particular time, that have to be thought again and again, and also because some of the thinker has to remain outside the thought in order for him or her to have it. In short, the eternal thoughts of the philosopher have to be realized in transient psychological contents, in the distracted moments of our lives.

The demand that we should, eventually, stand still, like a kestrel at stoop, on a definitive, all-encompassing thought seems even more absurd when we remind ourselves what it is like "in there" where we humans have our thoughts. Anyone who has read James Joyce's *Ulysses* will have been reminded how our mental life consists of a torrent of fragments that seems closer to delirium than to contemplation; and this is true even when we are philosophizing. We overlook this because we think of philosophical thoughts as neat sentences, sitting nice and still on the page, not tossed all over the place, fading and dissolving, brightening and crystallizing, as they are in our living, endlessly distracted, multiply engaged, constantly interrupted consciousnesses. No wonder it is easier to reach conclusions than to dwell in them. And yet without this aim, philosophizing easily degenerates into a shopping expedition in a cognitive mall.

What philosophy in the end demands of us is *concentration*, and of a different kind from that which enables us to formulate, or follow, a complex argument. To think "Being is" or even really to think about the nature of mind (which will include the mind that is currently thinking – Marcel's point again) or to think about thought (which includes the thoughts that are being thought) requires the kind of discipline that we associated with mystics. And this is something that pretty well everything in our life, in which we surf attractions and distractions, militates against. According to Heidegger, the most thought-provoking feature "in our thought-provoking time is that we are still not thinking" (1968: 6). This paradoxical claim certainly seems true when our cogitations are measured against his notion of what it is truly to think philosophically: "to confine yourself to a single thought that one day stands like a star in the world's sky".

Philosophers (or, at least, metaphysicians) endeavour to ascend from particular engagements of the mind to an overview of everything; but this breaks down to occurrent thoughts, to precisely those particular moments of engagement they are trying to rise above. Philosophy, which aims to be cognitively least parochial, boils down to local instances. The dancing token thought fails to achieve the thought-type; the psychological experience falls short of the stasis that is true arrival in thought. In this sense, the great thoughts of philosophy, those that purport to wrap up all that we are, and seem to offer the possibility of transcending the hungering, empirical self, and ascending into generality, are like the Promised Land: they enable us to catch a glimpse of a place in which we cannot dwell. Such glimpses are precious – perhaps some of the most precious things that life affords us – but do not ultimately free us from the treadmill of our wants. The impossibility of reaching the asymptote of philosophical thought is reflected in the joke of the Hegelian philosopher asserting that the entire world is one thought and that he is thinking it.

And with this joke, our quest to find a solution to the fourth hunger and an end to hunger, and to the hunger for hunger that comes in the wake of satiety, itself comes to an end.

5. Ending hunger

Therefore take no thought, saying What shall we eat? Or,
What shall we drink? Or, Wherewithal shall we be clothed?
(Matthew 6:31)

But seek ye first the kingdom of God, and his righteousness;
and all these things shall be added unto you. (Matthew 6:33)

Seek for food and clothing first, then the Kingdom of God
shall be added unto you. (Hegel [1807] 1977)

The hunger of others

In the time it takes to read this sentence, another person (most
probably a child) will have succumbed to starvation. Every hour
there are 1,000 deaths from hunger or from diseases to which the
malnourished body is prone. The 3,000 or so people whose deaths
in the 9/11 attack have had such an impact on the lives of people
in the West were a fraction of those who died from hunger on
that very day. What is more, for an eighth of the world's population, some 820,000,000 people, hunger is a permanent companion
(Vernon 2007)

For most of us, for most of the time, other people's starvation is
of little concern and is readily eclipsed by concern with the pursuit
of pleasure, the fortunes of our football team, or unhappy love. For

many, perhaps, it is of no concern at all. For only a few (to use Keats's words in "The Fall of Hyperion"), "the miseries of the world / Are Misery, and will not let them rest". Surely, one might think, if we, the well-fed, had an ounce of humanity, the daily torture and premature death of the malnourished should be a constant preoccupation. Even Brecht's apparently cynical aphorism "Grub first, then ethics" suggests that once the grub has been provided, ethics will follow. And there could be no more basic ethic than our obligation to those who lack the means to life.

Of course, things are not that simple. It is difficult to feel an ethical responsibility towards bare statistics. Most of us, coming upon a child dying of hunger in the street, would feel impelled to act; to drop whatever we were doing, however inconvenient, and do whatever necessary to save the child. This is in part because this is such a rare event. If undernourished children were an everyday spectacle, and if they do their dying (as they tend to do) out of sight, then the impulse to act would eventually wear out. (As tourists, we know how quickly unsolicited shocking spectacles become an irritating background to the ones we have paid to see.) Besides, we have our own lives to live, our own children to feed, our own responsibilities to others. And these priorities feel even more secure if what we are presented with is not a dying child but facts, garnished by the occasional image of a child in a world that one finds difficult to imagine.

There are other reasons why we, the well-fed, do not fret as much as might be expected about the hungry. The first is a feeling of hopelessness. The very scale of the problem makes any contribution we might ourselves make seem pitifully small. The second is uncertainty about the right thing to do. We have heard how donations of money end in the wrong hands, how airlifted food drops into the wrong mouths, how aid often serves only to enrich kleptocratic leaders who are thereby further empowered to oppress, terrorize and steal from their peoples. The solution to the problem, we conclude, lies not with us, who live in the wealthy countries far from the trouble, but with the well-off in those countries where starvation is so prevalent. They alone can build the structures that will ensure good governance, accountability and transparency, so that aid will actually help those who need it most. Steps to impose this as a precondition to aid are regarded by some as "patronizing", the continuation of colonialism by other means. At this stage, a fledgling sense of responsibility to the hungry starts to fade.

Our rationalized indifference is not unexpected. As James Vernon (to whom I owe the facts in the first paragraph) points out, concern for the hungry is a relatively modern phenomenon:

> There was a time, not so long ago, when the spectre of starvation was not disturbing and the plight of the hungry commanded little attention and no sympathy. Less than two hundred years ago hunger was considered either a natural condition or an inevitable and necessary one, beyond the government of man. Then the hungry were considered not fully human, despite often being objects of Christian charity; they were figures of opprobrium and disgust, not sympathy. Their hunger, and their vulnerability to acts of nature or providence, illustrated only their lack of industry and moral fibre. Then hunger was seen as a good and necessary thing: it taught the lazy and indulgent the moral discipline of labour; it taught them how to enter modernity as industrious individuals capable of competing in a market economy and providing for their families. (2007: 1–2)

This, then, rather than concern for our starving brethren, has been the default position throughout history. And it is not surprising; for even the well-fed had memories of hunger themselves and for the most part lived not too far above subsistence.

Vernon cites Piero Camporesi's vision "of a famished early modern Europe and its fevered alimentary imagination":

> In the centuries between the Renaissance and the Enlighten-ment, the continent of Europe was gripped by hunger. Processions of emaciated beggars and vagrants struggled to stay on their feet, scavenging and stealing, passing the rotting corpses of those who had stopped to rest and had not gotten up again. The survivors kept ceaselessly on the move in quest of work they were too weak to do. (*Ibid*.:10)

Against this background, and periodic famines subsequently, it is hardly surprising that people did not wish to identify with those who were malnourished, even less to share their crust with them, outside the highly structured charitable support systems and, in the circumstances remarkable, specific traditions of hospitality to strangers. Every act of generosity would bring you nearer to the threshold at which you, too, might tip over into irreversible decline. A concern for the hungry, other than those for whom you were responsible, such as your spouse and children, bordered on the imprudent, eating into the reserves you needed to store up against a rainy day.

For this reason, charity may not only begin but also end at home. Charles Dickens's Mrs Jellaby, concerned about the starving of Africa while her own children are neglected, is a compelling exem-plar and warning. Bernard Williams mounted a powerful critique of utilitarianism on related grounds (Smart & Williams 1973). If the aim of all our actions were to promote the greatest happiness of the greatest number, without favouring our own – so that we would rank the needs of our own children along with those of the children of strangers – we should fly in the face of all that has made society tolerable. The extended selfishness of our concern prima-rily with ourselves and our nearest and dearest makes a sounder basis for civilization, he argues, than an abstract concern for others shaped entirely by a Benthamite felicific calculus, in which we regard ourselves as mere conduits for a collective agency targeting the maximization of happiness. The terrifying example of totalitarian states, where only the *nomenklatura* are permitted to favour their own interests and that of their dependents, is a warning on a greater scale. The less terrifying, but nonetheless worrying, application of a remorselessly consistent utilitarianism in Peter Singer's (1973) attack on "speciesism" and his argument for giving preferential treatment to healthy apes over seriously handicapped children, should make us less critical of the extended egotism of our preferential concern for the needs of those whom we know over the needs of strangers, even if the needs of the latter are greater.

Even so, indifference to hungry strangers, the attitude of most people throughout most of history, is no longer justified for most of us in the affluent West. We live a long way above subsistence and there is a net to catch us if we fall. And we cannot plead ignorance: global communication systems table-serve the news of other peoples' hunger and the images of the starving inhabit our living rooms. And yet our concern with the hunger of others has not grown to occupy the space freed up by having a secure supply of food to meet our own hungers. And this is because, as we have seen throughout this book, this space is not empty. Other hungers take their place; which is why we are receptive to arguments absolving us of responsibility towards the hungry on the grounds that their problems lie within themselves or cannot, for other reasons, be relieved by us. And, even if we were persuaded that we can help, and that the best way to do it would be through properly audited government-managed overseas aid, the suggestion that a 10 per cent tax hike might be necessary would be sufficient to ensure non-election for the party that made it. And while in principle we might be sympathetic to the notion of tilting the terms of trade with less developed countries in their favour, or making them slightly less unfavourable, this sympathy would not withstand serious inroads into our spending.

In short, our out-of-control hungers make us relatively impervious to the hungers of others, especially distant others who come to our attention as statistics illustrated by emblematic images. This is one of the reasons why, throughout this book, I have focused on the metamorphoses of hunger beyond its biological base, rather than on the *prima facie* more important topic of the ethics of hunger in a world where many have little or nothing to eat while many more are eating far too much and are in hot pursuit of a multitude of secondary and elective hungers. If we do not understand the proliferation of hungers, and see how it fits into a broader picture of what it is to be a human being, we shall not make progress in taking seriously the hunger of others.

The hierarchy of hungers

Part of the problem of "downsizing" our needs is that our hungers are all tightly interconnected. To this extent, the division of hunger into biological hunger, hedonistic hunger, the hunger for others and the fourth or spiritual hunger, is somewhat artificial. The protean manifestations of hunger break out of the labelled boxes into which we have tried to confine them. The hunger of the collector may be rooted in part in atavistic echoes of the hunter and gatherer, and the prudence of the forebears preparing for famine at a time of plenty. It will also have something in it of the indirect assertion of power over others. What else are assets than the possibility of gaining a purchase on the human world? Even if we reject the Freudian interpretation of the obsessionality in the passion of the collector – hoarding as an expression of the constipation cultivated by the infant to manipulate its mother by withholding from her the primordial gift of the well-formed stool – it is easy to see how the passion directed towards the pursuit, capture and retention of the prized item may be displaced from the thwarted love of others. Self-aggrandisement through conspicuous consumption and the expansion of the asset register is another way of exercising at least symbolic power. The very fetishization of commodities – at its most intense expression in the collector's passion – is a way of possessing others, by possessing their labour, their skill, their craftsmanship, their time. There is also something of the artist in the collector: the completed set brings the aesthetic pleasure of the perfect form, in which each item belongs to a whole. And the ambition of the philosopher to make the world mind-portable is recognizable in the collector who, in the microcosm of the completed set, assembles a symbol of the macrocosm. The lifelong passion of the collector also binds together the days of his life: it speaks to the fourth hunger by lifting him above Humean series of experiences and "The Dominion of And".

Other hungers likewise refuse to be neatly confined to the chapters to which they have been assigned. As we saw, the volunteers in Keys's experiment displaced their biological hunger into an appetite for consumer goods: their miserable, malnourished state tried to comfort itself with second-hand clothes, knick-knacks, junk, old books in (to use Russell's words) "a bizarre ritual for compensation" (Russell 2006: 126). The hungers for others as expressed in sexual desire can become a near-animal longing for rutting; or be commodified as purchasable pleasure; or be a means of dominating others through humiliation; or be transformed (as in *Tristan und Isolde*) into a longing for the infinite, for something quite ethereal, for another world – the theme of much art. Many of our pleasures and pastimes are competitive and offer satisfaction (short-lived, of course) of the desire to conquer others, if only symbolically. As well as serving the elevated purposes we ascribed to it in Chapter 4, art itself may be a source of quite simple, sensual pleasure – indeed, it has been argued that food may be considered an art object – or a means of attracting members of the opposite sex, or of asserting power, or of making a living; and art appreciation can be reduced to the acquisition of collectors' items. The preference for one brand of nutritionally identical food over another may be rooted in a desire to broadcast a certain kind of identity, which makes the same flavour taste better when embedded in a particular nexus of associated ideas. The hunger for nutrition, for sensual pleasure, for power or an approving smile, and for wholeness and significance and inexhaustible meaning, are all mixed up in us and may morph into one another with dizzying facility. This should not perhaps surprise, when we think of how layered and folded our world is and how layered and folded are we who have our being in, and opposed to, that world.

This is not entirely to subvert the hierarchy implicit in the sequence of chapters, the sense of an ascent up a ladder of hungers that take us further and further away from the animal grubbing in the dirt for edible life that will support its own life. Admittedly this may be overturned – as in the case of drug addicts or those in whom the spiritual quest or the pursuit of knowledge overrides everything, when the basic means to life becomes less important than the pursuit of their passion. Civilisation began, according to W. H. Auden, with "the first flaker of flints / who forgot his dinner" ("Sexts"). And, on a lighter note, W. C. Fields reports how during a trip through Afghanistan, the party lost its corkscrew and thereafter suffered the hardship of being "compelled to live on food and water". Generally, however, the hierarchy holds up and it is a question of (again to quote Brecht) "grub first, then ethics" and certainly "grub first, then aesthetics" or "grub first, then hobbies", as in Hegel's inversion of Matthew: "Seek for food and clothing first, then the Kingdom of God shall be added unto you". The fasting saint and the artist dying of malnutrition for his art are the awe-inspiring exceptions that remind us of the rule.

Levi's testimony here is, as always, worthy of careful attention and, as always, complex. The hunger of malnutrition dominates everything: "The Lager [the camp] is hunger: we ourselves are hunger, living hunger" (1993: 74). And yet, amid the wall-to-wall horror, in which unremitting selfishness and calculation seemed necessary for survival, there was room for goodness; for example, the "pure and uncontaminated" humanity of Lorenzo, who "was outside this world of negation". It was thanks to Lorenzo, Levi says, that "I managed not to forget that I myself was a man" (*ibid.*: 122). By his example, Lorenzo demonstrated that there was such a thing as an impulse to be human that cut deeper even than hunger. And astonishingly, in a sea of hunger, cold, disease, violence and crushing work, Levi himself becomes preoccupied with remembering some lines from the Divine Comedy, which he is translating into French for a fellow prisoner. "I would give today's soup", he says, "to know how to connect 'the like on any day' to the last lines". On the other hand, the hierarchy of hungers asserts itself when, in the relative (very relative) comfort of the chemical laboratory to which he has been assigned, he becomes shamefully aware of his appalling physical appearance – his smell, the rags that passed for clothes, his cachexia – in the presence of the female laboratory assistants. His blood freezes when, asking one of the girls for advice, he is ignored and he hears her refer to him as "*Stink-jude*". There is a new, painful space, outside of the all-consuming hunger and cold, disease, violence and fear. Elsewhere, he meditates on our hungers outside of this *anus mundi*:

For human nature is such that grief and pain – even simultaneously suffered – do not add up as a whole in our consciousness, but hide, the lesser behind the greater, according to a definite law of perspective. It is providential and is our means of surviving in the camp. And this is the reason why so often in free life one hears it said that a man is never content. In fact it is not a question of a human incapacity for a state of absolute happiness, but an ever-insufficient knowledge of the

complex nature of the state of unhappiness; so that the single
name of the major cause is given to all its causes, which are
composite and set out in an order of urgency. And if the most
immediate cause of stress comes to an end, you are grievously
amazed to see that another one lies behind; and in reality a
whole series of others. (Levi 1993: 73)

From this, the testimony of one of the most profound witnesses to
human nature, we may arrive at the Socratic wisdom of knowing
how little we know. We do not know ourselves; we do not know
what we want.

We shall not reach a complete understanding of our hungers, at
first sight the most obvious aspect of our humanity, because they
rest on something that, as we pointed out at the beginning, is deeply
mysterious. Fully to understand our hungers we would have to have
a satisfactory account of the place of conscious experience in the
natural world and, more specifically, of the emergence of elaborate,
sustained, self-consciousness in human beings. There is no obvious
explanation why consciousness (instead of better mechanisms) has
evolved in certain branches of the evolutionary tree or of how it has
emerged out of the material world. It does not seem like a sensible
idea, especially since the contents of consciousness do not correspond to anything that exists in the material world. The sensations
associated with hunger are not the "low-down" or the "inside story"
of the material state of the hungry organism; even less the "inside
surface" of the distance between the state the organism is in and
the state it should be in. And self-consciousness, the matrix out of
which so many of our hungers have grown, is equally, perhaps more,
mysterious. It seems such a small thing for consciousness to turn
back on itself and for a conscious being to become a self-conscious
one; one that feels, says, and worries over "I". But of course it is
not: the assumption of something as *itself*, so that it knows that it
exists and that it is itself, cannot be accommodated in the third-

person (or strictly no-person) world of the physical or biological sciences. It is because we are self-conscious that we live in, and in relation to, a *world* – a human and natural world had in common – and have a sense of our life course. Here our hungers breed and multiply and proliferate and give rise to the dreams and longings that consume us. Our hungers, then, are rooted in mystery. Hunger is the paramount expression of the mysterious burden (or gift) of consciousness and the even more mysterious burden (or gift) of human consciousness.

We may, however, safely conclude that to be human is always to be in the grip of some kind of hunger, if only for hunger itself. We can fool our desires or outflank them by engaging in a multiplicity of intermediate activities with a distant relationship to an ill-conceived goal and by this means palliate our hunger for hunger, our fundamental appetite for appetite itself. But this may in the end seem unsatisfactory: a mode of self-forgetting that does not fully answer to our sense of possibility – the possibility of joy, of happiness, of completion, or at least of self-realization. The question then arises as to how, individually and collectively, we may manage our hungers: individually so that we are not perpetually eaten from within by what we feel are unmet needs, by lacks, by ever-proliferating wants and wants arising out of wants; and collectively so that we shall not destroy each other, in a competition for resources to fuel spiralling needs and support a rising curve of consumption, thereby leaching the planet of the sum total of its beneficence.

Making others hungry

The first step towards managing our hungers must be to see, if not to understand, their nature: to comprehend that they are potentially infinite and that hungering man cannot ultimately be satisfied. We need to be more conscious of the way in which our hungers are fuelled and this includes being aware of how individually and collectively we exacerbate each other's hungers.

Man has replaced nature as the chief agent of human hunger. Famines such as those in Bengal are only the most dramatic example of how it is not always natural disasters that perpetuate hunger but more often the way we order our affairs collectively. There are the inadvertent consequences of our rising curve of consumption, and no consumption is entirely without what economists would call "externalities". This is seen most dramatically in the adverse impact on the developing world of meeting the demands of developed countries. To take an example that is of current concern, the push to biofuels – intended to reconcile the desire to continue consuming energy at an undiminished rate with limiting carbon emissions – diverts food grown in economically undeveloped countries from the stomachs of the poor to the petrol tanks of the rich. More broadly, the requirement for cheap food and consumer goods means that developed countries will defend terms of trade that are unfavourable to developing countries.

While the origin of our consumer choices seems to lie inside us, we are subject to social pressures encouraging us to develop and satisfy new hungers. This was a much debated theme in the middle years of the twentieth century when, in various ways, Galbraith, Packard and the Frankfurt School of Social Research (whose ideas were popularized by writers such as Marcuse, although as we saw earlier they were anticipated by Hegel) made clear how affluent societies were increasingly characterized by the pressures within them to drive increasing consumption. The implantation of needs for consumer goods was so effective that people felt defined by the objects they bought and they experienced the need for consumer items – remote from any kind of primary necessity – as keenly as they had hitherto felt the need for the wherewithal for survival. Being possessed by socially legitimized, indeed mandated, needs is a striking manifestation of the false or alienated consciousness

Marx spoke of. These trends have become ever more apparent in the half century since we first became aware of the power of the "hidden persuaders". Increasingly intense collective self-consciousness, made possible by the ubiquity of the media, has meant that the Spinozean truth that "we desire that which we see others desire" is ever more active in our lives: we see more of others' desires and their objects. Celebrity culture, which values individuals for being famous, values them, in short, for being valued, confers on celebrities the authority to define the desirable life. An endless flow of images and stories gives non-celebrities a benchmark against which to measure how their own lives are falling short. This is simply the most potent manifestation of the influences that persuade us to want more and more and more, if only to offset a feeling of being somehow inferior in an unequal society. While we still retain some capacity to measure ourselves against our immediate fellows and do acknowledge that those who (as Yeats said of kings) live out others' dreams are themselves unreal, a celebrity culture, by legitimizing, indeed sacralizing, a certain kind of success attached to high consumption, is an important source of fuel for turbo-capitalism.

The need to be envied by others goes very deep. As Gore Vidal said, "It is not enough to succeed. Others must fail". Our hungers are exacerbated by the desire to awaken hungers in others – effectively to impoverish them. Conspicuous consumption is only the most obvious manifestation of this but there are other ways in which we may contribute to making others hungry. We have already mentioned how frenzied consumption in developed countries may distort the economies of developing countries with impoverishing consequences. Nearer to home, there is the adverse impact of widening disparities in income, which goes beyond the damage caused by the dubious means by which the wealthy acquired their wealth. Their purchasing power may drive up prices in the UK, the housing market being the most obvious example. There are complex psychosocial "externalities" that help to explain why well-being and happiness have not apparently grown in parallel with *per capita* income. Societies in which there are greater disparities in disposable income are overall unhappier than those that have the same average *per capita* income and lesser economic disparities. The rich do not enrich their own lives and they impoverish the lives of others.

There are other areas where our hungers are exacerbated by others and where satisfying them *requires* the hunger of others. We saw how, for Hegel, our hunger for others required an unreciprocated acknowledgement: my satisfaction seemed to depend on the other's abjection, although it was frustrated by this. The happy cooperation of companionate love was found to conceal at its heart a flight from what was essentially a fight to the death. At a less metaphysical level, self-esteem in the sphere of sexual relations seems to depend, for some at least, on breaking hearts as well as having relations with many partners. At an only slight less reprehensible level, there is a kind of carelessness among those who are sexually successfully about the psychological externalities of their behaviour. This passage from Nicholas Shakespeare's biography of the charismatic writer Bruce Chatwin is very much to the present point. Chatwin's mesmerizing presence and physical beauty made him intensely sexually attractive with unhappy consequences for most of those who were attracted, as Shirley Conran observed:

A lot of people were in love with Bruce and I'm sorry for all of them. I saw the misery it brought. We have all loved people and left them, but when Bruce danced on to the next he had the ability to leave them empty and bereft in a way I doubt they ever recovered from. He'd wander carelessly in and out of someone's life in an afternoon and they'd be dazzled for the rest of their lives.   (Shakespeare 1999: 494)

In this, as in so many other spheres, the constraints of the law and the internalized disapproval of others are not sufficient to prevent our satisfaction of our own hungers awakening damaging hungers in others.

Affluent societies whose members are eaten up with ambition, competition, jealousy, unrequited longing for recognition, love, or sexual conquest, may be deaf to the basic hungers of the wretched of the earth, even if they accept their own role in making them wretched. That is why we should be aware of the extent to which deliberately, accidentally or even unconsciously, we fuel the hungers of others. While those hungers may, in some souls possessed by grace or a steely self-discipline, be sublimated into a life dedicated to some worthwhile cause – a favourite theme of literature – it is more often the case that those who are themselves consumed with hunger will find little time for the hunger of others.

The solution may seem to lie at the political level but we have to be on our guard. The events of the twentieth century spelt out in grisly detail the sometimes appalling consequences of a politics fuelled by envy that pretended to take us beyond envy. The sense of outrage that some live in the lap of luxury while others lack the barest necessities, when it is translated into violent political action that results in power being concentrated in the hands of the *enragés*, usually has catastrophic consequences as we know only too well from the history of communism. The violent rectification of injustices led to greater injustices. The rhetoric of "justice for all" justified unspeakable injustices imposed on those increasing numbers of individuals who seemed to be less than wholeheartedly committed to the cause – the Ukrainian kulaks, for example, and by association the entire population of Ukraine. We should be aware of the dangers of the politics that deny the reality of envy and the reality of the all-too-human desire to inflame the hungers of those who do not have what we have. Egalitarian rhetoric has often been a smokescreen for a new order in which some (fewer than before the revolution) enjoyed luxuries while many (more than before the revolution) lacked for basic necessities.

We should be suspicious of the pretence that we do not for at least some of the time *need* the hunger of others, if only as consolation for our own unrequited hunger for others. And we have to acknowledge that all of us are too caught up in our own hungers – for all that they may be expressed indirectly, as in an addiction to televised sport – to attend to the hungers of others with the seriousness that they deserve. While we would hope that our political systems express what is best, rather than what is worst, in us, any system that denies these truths about us is likely to become a moralized tyranny, and to be riddled with hypocrisy. To override this fact about humanity by an inflicted utilitarianism that pretends that we are as concerned about ourselves collectively as we are about ourselves individually, about the anonymous mass of strangers as about our nearest and dearest, and that we are proportionately concerned about things that are objectively urgent, so that we will place the need to feed the masses in front of our own need to have a good time, is to court disaster.

One of the most poisonous of all the toxins arising from the communist dictatorships was the imposition of the rhetoric of communal concern on public discourse. The fact that those who imposed it did so in order that they might exert thought control, so that their self-interests could be pursued with less hindrance, made it all the more corrosive of true solidarity. In the impassioned Introduction to her *Café Europa: Life After Communism*, the Croatian writer Slavenka Draculić described her almost visceral loathing of the obligatory use of the first-person plural "we" in every utterance. No one was allowed to speak for himself or herself or in his or her own person but always had to speak on behalf of the collective, in the voice of the collective that marched in parallel, that spoke as one, in which each pretended to subordinate their own interests to that of the all. The results – corruption, oppression, hatred, in short, public life reduced to a concentration camp for the mind and, often, the body – are too well-known to need spelling out. The reality behind compulsory we-speak was expressed in the degradation of public spaces, in the appalling standards of public services and a profound indifference of each towards that community of potentially murderous strangers that formed the general public. This is a grim commentary on the Hegelian communitarian ideas that lay at the very root of Marxism; on the pious belief that public duty, far from being a restriction on liberty, would actually be liberating and that freedom might lie in conformity to the ethos of an organic community. The result – "slave camps under the flag of freedom" (in the words of Albert Camus) – is entirely predictable to anyone who has meditated on human hungers. The central presupposition of utopia – that our hungers will somehow serve our fellow men and not set one against another, that there are fundamental desires that will drive us to work for the common good rather than pursue our selfish ends – must not be abandoned. But we must surely be cautious in how we think about persuading ourselves and others to make the hungers of others a priority.

Sustainable non-growth

Let us not be defeatist. We have no right, after all, to assume a self-serving despair that denies hope to the destitute. Let us suppose that we can collectively arrive at a state in which we are sufficiently free of our own hungers of affluence to be prepared to address the hungers of the malnourished by becoming less single-mindedly consumerist. Thinking about how we may achieve this, in particular how we might wean ourselves individually and collectively from the impulse to consume, and from the treadmill of pleasure and self-indulgence, raises certain questions to which there are no clear answers. Successive generations of students and others in the

1960s, 1970s and 1980s, who subscribed so noisily to a counter-culture of resistance to implanted wants, and seemingly wished to bring down a capitalist system that demanded endless growth and fuelled an ever-rising demand for goods, seem themselves to have evolved into consumers on a scale hardly imagined by their parents. The problem is a collective one and against such a problem the individual feels impotent and the collective has no clearly defined collective will, except that expressed through certain very blunt and intermittently used instruments such as the ballot box. Individual acts of "downshifting" are difficult, and anyway tend to be less radical than they appear. Just as few of us could afford to live in the kind of poverty, the conspicuous non-consumption, that Ghandi chose, so "downshifting", "dropping out" and so on usually presuppose a background of wealth, a reliance on others to continue to provide the infrastructure of what we take for granted as civilized life. They are possible without serious hardship only if the bonfires of capitalism continue to burn on. One can drop out of part of the system while still remaining very much inside most of it; and this is true of those trying to consume less. They still consume, involuntarily, on a massive scale.

Even if these obstacles to reducing consumption were overcome, there are other potential problems. In his famous *Fable of the Bees*, Bernard de Mandeville (1729) argued that the economic activity associated with vice, cheating, knavery, lust, luxury and so on was essential to a healthy state. Remove vice and the pursuit of luxury, and the engines of the economy would grind to a halt; poverty, destitution and a state vulnerable to predators and invasion would follow. Mandeville's fable reflects the very widespread feeling that any attempt to reduce growth will threaten the very fabric of a society whose sense of its own health relies on feeling that it is growing. Economic policy since the Second World War has been obsessed with growth, encapsulated most succinctly in Margaret Thatcher's TINA ("There is no alternative") principle. A non-growing economy is seen as a stagnant economy and stagnation as the road to rot. The possibility of recession and unemployment is brought nearer by a loss of confidence that propels a downward spiral. Even if non-growth were healthy, even necessary, as I have suggested, it would not be *seen* as such and, given that perceptions are one of the major determinants of economic trends, economic malaise would follow. There have even been suggestions that economic growth is a positive moral force, making people more open, more tolerant, more confident. The sociologist Max Weber and after him R. H. Tawney suggested that historically growth has had a theological resonance: the amassment of wealth was evidence of one's salvation. The work ethic, transformed into a growth ethic, was a spiritual principle. Better, anyway, to go for growth than to allow the people to relapse into the status of vulnerable lotus eaters, subsisting on an easily acquired sufficiency.

This notwithstanding, the case against growth is mounting as its adverse consequence become more evident and its supposed benefits look more questionable. Growth produces more inequality than prosperity, more insecurity than genuine progress. Most of the gains have accrued to a small minority at the top. In the US, for example, after an extraordinarily sustained period of growth, there is more inequality now than at any time since the Gilded Age, when rampant capitalism placed vast sums of money in the hands of a brutal and unscrupulous minority. Increasingly, it is being noted that inequalities do not even increase the happiness of those at the top of the heap and, as we have already noted, the impact of the wealthy on the rest of the population is decisively negative. For the majority, the comparators are getting worse. (That is why in communist countries, according to Draculić, people were always taught to look at people who were worse off than themselves rather than, say, the *nomenklatura* or those in the West who were better off.)

Economic growth is relatively recent, as the great economist John Maynard Keynes pointed out. It began, after 2,000 years of steady state, with the invention of the steam engine early in the eighteenth century. This created the demand for fossil fuels – in the first instance coal – and those supplies, which took many millions of years to create, are now beginning to run out. At the same time, the mounting problem of terrestrial and atmospheric pollution arising out of burning such fuel is increasingly evident. We seem to be coming to the end of what Bill McKibben has described as "a onetime gift that underwrote a onetime binge of growth" (2007). We need to look for graceful ways of slowing down; of finding a means of soft landing. We need a new kind of war on want: a war on wanting, on the want that wants even if it cannot define what it is that it wants. This war begins within ourselves and an understanding of our hungers – of their insatiability – or of the hungers that come in the wake of satiety.

This is not an argument against having more than one, strictly, needs. In this respect we are at one with King Lear. What is more, the metamorphoses of our endless hunger, the awakening of hungers by which we define ourselves that go beyond the hungers that seem to be given by our status as organisms, are central to our greatness. The drive of the well-fed to different kinds of consumption, not to speak of the hunger to go beyond consumption that misunderstands itself and gets expressed in, or settles for, more consumption, is one of the great motors to human advancement. If Eros is, as Auden said in his elegy for Freud, the "builder of cities", hunger has been the creator of our civilization. And the well-fed have tended their "higher hungers" at a time when many of their fellow beings have been condemned to abject starvation. This is inevitable; if we waited for everyone to be well-fed before we considered it entirely proper to attend to the hungers of the spirit, humanity would have been deprived of art, philosophy, most of science (which is largely curiosity-driven) and consequently science-based technology. The unparalleled legacy left to us by the Greeks was achieved at a time when only a minority of the population of Athens was properly fed and at least a third were formally enslaved. Sophocles' explorations of the meaning of life through the vehicle of tragedy were written when, for most people, tragedy consisted of early death through starvation and neglect, rather than hubris-engendered nemesis or being tricked by angry gods into sleeping with one's mother. History, what is more, has many cunning passages. Precisely those pursuits that have seemed most remote from pressing human need have often ultimately delivered most to alleviate those needs. The supreme example in this respect is that of Parmenides, whose poem that dismisses all experience as illusion has indirectly inspired not only metaphysics but also reason-based enquiry and, more broadly, science and consequently the science-based technology that has done more than anything else to alleviate hunger. Over a wider front, great egocentrics, narrowly focused on the objects of their hunger, have brought great blessings as well as great horrors on the world. (Unfortunately, as affluence has liberated more of us – including those of us whose horizons are otherwise low – more ape the behaviour of the talented, driven egocentrics who changed things for better or worse.)

We need to find a middle path, in the case of our lower hungers at least, between altruistic renunciation – few of us after all are prepared to undergo downsizing even to the extent of accepting significant rises in taxes, or a serious pegging back of lifestyle – and the unchecked pursuit of unlimited consumption. One such middle path would be to embrace and perfect those pleasures that we have, such that we would not have to set out on a career of endless further pleasures. To find in our daily bread the transcendence that we seek; and thus to agree, at least in part, with Epicurus, who in his *Letter on Happiness* claimed that "The beginning and root of all good is the pleasure of the stomach; even wisdom and culture must be referred to this" (quoted in Symons 2007: 19). The Slow Food Movement, launched in Italy as a protest against the establishment of a McDonald's restaurant in the Piazza di Spagna in Rome, would have won his approval as a starting place for a new approach to life. Advocating the enjoyment of food derived from local produce and cooked and eaten with love and care, it generalized to the Slow Movement, an informal organization committed to promoting "slowness, reflection and togetherness". The World Institute of Slowness has a vision of a slow planet, which would have won the approval of Ruskin: "it does a man, if he be truly a man, no harm to go slow: for his glory is not at all in going, but in being" (Reeves 2007: 132). Consistent with its ethos, the institute recommends that people wishing to convert to Slow Lives should "start slowly"!

An obvious route to conversion would be a focus on how one might experience one's experiences, and how one might learn truly to count as blessings the riches that are available in the most ordinary of lives. One aspect of this would be to try really to possess the numerous possessions we have; to wonder at the ingenuity and complexity of the artefacts that furnish and service our hours; to unpack all that goes into the miracle of the most ordinary moment. Compiling the most casual register of the assets that fill one's house and garden and life and rejoicing in the many-layered complexity of the town or city in which one dwells would be a start. From this beginning – a growing appreciation of one's life – it might be possible to cultivate an almost mystical joy at being the centre of the revelation that is the world spread out before one; or even to delight in the mere fact of one's existence, in the precious hours of daylight between eternity-thick walls of darkness. To think in this way would truly be an act of thanksgiving, open to believers and unbelievers alike.

Hungry to the end?

Who knows, perhaps such reflections may make the affluent less avid for new possessions, new experiences, new pastimes and new sexual partners. Thus liberated from the treadmill of their own hungers, the well-fed may find more space within their lives and hearts to concern themselves with the direct and unremitting hungers of those whose journey through life is largely the history of the sensations of a starving body. Could we then look forward to a time when biological hunger is eventually abolished from the face of the earth or, at least, from the experience of mankind? Would that be possible? And if it were possible would those liberated from the grinding misery of material privation be free only to suffer the other hungers that delight and torment their more fortunate fellow men? Could we look forward to a time when to be human is no longer to be hungry? Is this likely? Is it desirable?

Recall where we began: with the need to resist the restlessness of a material world, of which we are a part, although we are also apart from it. The stability of the living organism is not a given, a default state, mere inertia like that of a pebble. Life is therefore a constant struggle to maintain itself. The means by which life keeps itself alive get ever more complex, as is reflected in the evolution of nutrition from simple transactions, across the cellular membrane and within the cell, to all those physical processes and human actions that lead up to the laid table laden with dinner. The differentiation of cells is supplanted by the differentiation of structures and organs with different functions; the passive location of the organism is replaced by active positioning; active self-location becomes ever more purposive as behaviour to ensure positioning is more elaborate; the internal environment is regulated and then, increasingly, the external environment. Housing supplements homoeostatic mechanisms to maintain the temperature of our tissues within the range compatible with life.

All of these processes are present in human beings whose survival depends, as in the case of other living creatures, on a restlessness that counteracts the restlessness of the outside world that brought them into being but also threatens to destroy them. In human beings there is something else: a self-consciousness that makes purposive behaviour explicitly purposive; a consciousness of others that socializes hunger, both as a shared problem and as a merging of the nourishment of food and the deeply human nourishment of a personal relationship; and, arising out of this, an ability progressively to transform the environment to suit the needs of the organism and of the person, the embodied subject. We are at the end of a long journey that leads from the flagellae of micro-organisms, through monuments of instinct such as ant heaps and bird nests, to the great artefactscapes that are cities. But, at the heart of our lives, there remains a restlessness that is experienced as hunger, as appetite, as desire, as lack, as want, as a craving for wholeness. The living processes that are polyphasic systems in dynamic equilibrium are reflected at every level. To dismount from hunger is to dismount from life. Stasis is death.

This is acknowledged by Pascal, one of our key witnesses as to the origin and evolution of our hungers. While he asserts that "all men's misfortunes spring from the single cause that they are unable to stay quietly in one room" (1961: 83), he also notes that "Our nature is one of movement; to be completely still is to be dead" (*ibid.*). This restlessness is life itself; and human life is a higher restlessness. It is because human beings do not simply fall asleep after eating (and rutting) but are dissatisfied that (to quote Pascal again) "*L'homme passe infiniment l'homme*": man infinitely surpasses himself.

So what can we hope for? Will absence of hunger mean emptiness even if, by some ingenious means, we are saved from boredom? Is the man or woman less who, "all passion spent", is able at last to sit still in a room? What if our seemingly endless, restless becoming were able to end in the quiescence of Being? And if all mankind entered into this state, would the "divine discontent" that has taken us so far from our animal origins, which has driven human beings to such heights as well as to such depths of despair and individual and collective abomination, cease to drive us "onward and upwards"? Should we be glad if, after all, our hungers prove intrinsically insatiable?

For Sartre the aspiration to completeness, the fundamental project of the for-itself that is human consciousness to become an in-itself, is an endeavour to be our own foundation and to escape our contingency: this is impossible. He concludes that "Man is a useless passion" (1957: 615), a conclusion with which one may be more likely to concur after 615 pages of the often opaque prose of *Being and Nothingness*. What if man *is* a useless passion? Perhaps we should celebrate that very futility. Does this not make humankind's great achievements somehow more magnificent (just as cathedrals seem even greater to those of us who believe that the god in whose honour they were raised does not exist)? This is what Camus, Sartre's one-time friend and subsequently sworn enemy, celebrated in his great essay *The Myth of Sisyphus* (1975). It was Sisyphus' punishment for treating the gods with the contempt they deserved to have to pass his eternity in the underworld, deploying heroic efforts to roll a stone to the top of a mountain only to see it roll down the other side – again and again and again. For Camus, Sisyphus is the "absurd hero" in "his scorn of the gods, his hatred of death, and his passion for life".

We build things to our satisfaction, only to find that what we have built no longer answers to our needs. As Gottfried Benn put it in one of his last poems: "Life is the building of bridges / Over rivers that seep away" ("Epilog", in Benn 1961). The stone rolls down the hill again but, undaunted, we turn round and set off once more up the hill. But the journey is not quite the same: repetition is not quite repetition. Humanity continues to mark out hitherto untrodden paths, driven by hungers it thinks it understands but does not. "The struggle itself is enough to fill man's heart. One must imagine Sisyphus happy". To put this another way, life may be a futile passion but it is also beautiful.

The reader may recall the tautology, a lived tautology, that I suggested would come to haunt the one living creature that is aware of it: "Your life is first of all what may be lost / its ultimate end not to end" (Williams 2007). It is within the circle of that tautology that all hunger, even human hunger that seems remote from the concerns of all other living creatures, is experienced and satisfied or not.

And here we must end our philosophical enquiry into hunger. One purpose of philosophy is to make the obvious less obvious and to raise fundamental questions about how and for what we live. Kass's question "How does one truly nourish the hungry human soul?" (1999: xxi) is perhaps the most important facing man today. For a truly nourished human soul may be more concerned about the hungers of others. And the future health of the planet and of its human inhabitants depends on arriving at an answer that is true to the human condition: that of a creature that is part of nature and yet at an increasing distance from it. We need at any rate to think how we are to contain our hungers in a way that is both inwardly and outwardly sustainable; to learn how to live a life more abundant without jeopardizing the abundance of the lives of others; in short, to know and better understand and manage our hungers.

Further reading

The topic of hunger as envisaged in this book is almost boundless and the relevant bibliography therefore potentially infinite. My suggestions have been dictated by the particular approach I have taken to hunger. Another approach would have justified a different bibliography.

Two books should appear on any list: *Hunger* by Sharman Apt Russell (2006), a deeply human exploration of the experience, history and significance of hunger; and *The Hungry Soul* by Leo Kass (1999), whose rich and profoundly thoughtful exploration of feeding and eating is an *entrée* into the kind of philosophical anthropology to which the present book aspires. I am also indebted to *Food and Philosophy*, edited by Fritz Allhof and Dave Monroe (2007), a witty and wide-ranging collection that includes contributions from foodies, chefs and people who have recovered from eating disorders. James Vernon's detailed study of our changing attitudes to the hungry, *Hunger* (2007), is among other things a sobering reminder of the extent to which humanity, and inhumanity, rather than nature, is responsible for the malnutrition that is a life-sentence for so many.

The reader may wish to pick and mix from among the books that are listed in the Bibliography. The anti-scientistic (but *not* anti-scientific!) position taken in the present book, the philosophical anthropology that informs it and my particular "take'" on human consciousness have been set out *in extenso* in many of my own books, in particular the trilogy *The Hand* (2003), *I Am* (2004) and *The Knowing Animal* (2005). John Gray's *Straw Dogs* (2002), as muddled as it is misanthropic, is an excellent example of the posturing human self-hatred that is the implicit target of the present book.

Erwin Schrödinger's classic *What is Life?* (1992) has informed the ideas in the opening section. Primo Levi's *Survival in Auschwitz* (1993) is one of the greatest books of the twentieth century and Levi is a key witness to what hunger tells us about human nature. Pascal's *Pensées* – which have been cited throughout – are as illuminating to anyone, atheist or religious believer, trying to understand their own hungers. There are two translations (1961, [1966] 1995) and they have different virtues, which is why I have drawn on them both.

Although Chapter 3 depends very heavily on ideas drawn from Hegel's *Phenomenology of Spirit* ([1807] 1977) and Sartre's *Being and Nothingness* (1957), neither is recommended for the general reader. I have derived more understanding of Hegel from secondary sources – Kojéve, Camus and Sartre – but I would recommend Peter Singer's *Hegel* (1983) as a starting-point. And although my own copy of *Being and Nothingness* is heavily underlined throughout, I think his ontology is best approached through Arthur Danto's *Sartre* (1975). Thus prepared, the reader is then strongly recommended to try "Concrete Relations with Others", in particular the opening section "First Attitude Toward Others: Love, Language, Masochism". My own *The Knowing Animal* deals with the distinctive nature of human consciousness relevant to the contrast between appetite and desire. The final chapter of that book also discusses the "fourth hunger" in more detail.

Bibliography

Allhof, F. & D. Monroe 2007. *Food and Philosophy: Eat, Think and Be Merry.* Oxford: Blackwell.

Barthes, R. 1973. *Mythologies*, Annette Lavers (trans.). London: Paladin.

Barthes, R. 1978. *A Lover's Discourse: Fragments*, Richard Howard (trans.). New York: Hill & Wang.

Benn, G. 1961. *Primal Vision*, E. B. Ashton (ed.), M. Hamburger (trans.). London: Bodley Head.

Bentham, J. 1907. *Introduction to the Principles of Morals and Legislation.* Oxford: Clarendon Press. Available online, Library of Economics and Liberty, www.econlib.org/library/Bentham/bnthPMLContents.html (accessed April 2008).

Bradley F. H. [1876] 1962. *Ethical Studies.* Oxford: Oxford University Press.

Brown, M. 2007. "Picky Eating is a Moral Failure". See Allhof & Monroe (2007), 192–207.

Büchner, G. 1952. *Danton's Death.* In *The Plays of George Buchner*, Geoffrey Dunlop (trans.). London: Vision Press.

Camus, A. 1975. *The Myth of Sisyphus.* Harmondsworth: Penguin.

Conrad, J. 1960. *Heart of Darkness, Almayer's Folly, The Lagoon.* New York: Doubleday.

Danto, A. C. 1975. *Sartre.* London: Fontana.

Drakulić, S. 1996. *Café Europa: Life After Communism.* London: Abacus.

Eliot, T. S. 1954. *Ash Wednesday.* In his *Selected Poems.* London: Faber.

Gould, S. J. 1994 "The Evolution of Life on Earth". *Scientific American* (October).

Gray, J. 2002. *Straw Dogs: Thoughts on Humans and Other Animals.* London: Granta.

Hamsun, K. 2003. *Hunger*, George Egerton (trans.), www.gutenberg.org/etext/8387 (accessed April 2008).

Hastings, M. 2007. *Nemesis: The Battle for Japan, 1944–5.* London: Harper Press.

Hegel, G. W. F. [1807] 1977. *Phenomenology of Spirit*, A. V. Miller (trans.). Oxford: Oxford University Press.

Heidegger, M. 1968. *What is Called Thinking?*, Fred D. Wieck & J. Glenn Gray (trans.). New York: Harper.

Heller, E. 1961. *The Disinherited Mind: Essays in Modern German Literature and Thought.* Harmondsworth: Penguin.

Hodgson, D. 2008. "A Role for Consciousness". *Philosophy Now* **65**: 22–4.

Iggers, J. 2007. "Who Needs a Critic? The Standard of Taste and the Power of Branding". See Allhof & Monroe (2007), 88–101.

Jukes, M. 2004. *The Wine List 2004: The Top 250 Wines of the Year*. London: Headline.

Kass L. R. 1999. *The Hungry Soul: Eating and the Perfecting of Our Nature*. Chicago, IL: University of Chicago Press.

Keats, J. 1988. *Poems of 1820: And the Fall of Hyperion*, D. G. Gillham (ed.). Plymouth: Northcote House.

Kravchenko, V. 1946. "Harvest in Hell". In his *I Chose Freedom*. New York: Scribner.

Larkin, P. 1988. *Collected Poems*, Anthony Thwaite (ed.). London: Faber.

Layard, R. 2005. *Happiness: Lessons from a New Science*. Harmondsworth: Penguin.

Levi, P. 1993. *Survival in Auschwitz: The Nazi Assault on Humanity*, Stuart Woolf (trans.). New York: Simon & Schuster.

Lintott, S. 2007. "Sublime Hunger: A Consideration of Eating Disorders Beyond Beauty". See Allhoff & Monroe (2007), 58–70.

McMahon, D. 2005. *Happiness: A History*. New York: Atlantic Monthly Press.

McKibben, B. 2007. *Deep Economy: The Wealth of Communities and the Durable Future*. New York: Times Books/Henry Holt.

Mandeville, B. de 1732. *The Fable of the Bees. Or Private Vices, Publick Benefits*, 6th edn. London: J. Tonson. Available in digitized form at www.google.books.com

Marx K. & F. Engels 1974. *The German Ideology*, C. J. Arthur (ed.). London: Lawrence & Wishart.

Mill, J. S. 1989. *Autobiography*, J. M. Robson (ed.). Harmondsworth: Penguin.

Milosz, C. 1980. *The Captive Mind*, Jane Zielonko (trans.). Harmondsworth: Penguin.

Mithen, S. 2005. *The Prehistory of the Mind: A Search for the Origins of Art, Religion and Science*. London: Phoenix.

Nichols, S. & T. Grantham 2000. "Adaptive Complexity and Phenomenal Consciousness". *Philosophy of Science* **67**(4): 648–70.

Patočka, J. 2007. "Some Comments Concerning the Extramundane and Mundane Position of Philosophy". In *Jan Patočka: Living in Problematicity*, Eric Manton (trans.), 18–28. Prague: Oikoymenh.

Pascal, B. [1966] 1995. *Pensées*, A. J. Krailsheimer (trans.). Harmondsworth: Penguin.

Pascal, B. 1961. *Pensées*, J. M. Cohen (trans.). Harmondsworth: Penguin.

Pyle, A. (ed.) 1999. *Key Philosophers in Conversation: The Cogito Interviews*. London: Routledge.

Reeves, R. 2007. *John Stuart Mill: Victorian Firebrand*. London: Atlantic.

Russell, S. A. 2006. *Hunger: An Unnatural History*. New York: Basic Books.

Sacker, I. M. & M. A. Zimmer 1987. *Dying to be Thin: Understanding and Defeating Anorexia Nervosa and Bulimia*. New York: Warner.

Sartre, J.-P. 1957. *Being and Nothingness*, Hazel Barnes (trans.). London: Methuen.

Schopenhauer, A. 1969. *The World as Will and Representation*, E. F. J. Payne (trans.). New York: Dover.

Schrödinger, E. 1992. *What Is Life? The Physical Aspects of the Living Cell*. Cambridge: Cambridge University Press (Canto).

Shakespeare, N. 1999. *Bruce Chatwin*. London: Cape.

Singer, P. 1973. "Taking Life". In *Practical Ethics*, 2nd edn, 175–217. Cambridge: Cambridge University Press.

Singer, P. 1983. *Hegel: A Very Short Introduction*. Oxford: Oxford University Press.

Smart, J. J. C. & B. Williams 1973. *Utilitarianism: For and Against*. Cambridge: Cambridge University Press.

Spinoza, B. 1910. *Ethics and De Emendatione Intellectus*. London: Everyman.

Stadnyuk, I. 1963. *People are not Angels* London: Arthur Barker.

Symons, M. 2007. "Epicurus, the Foodies' Philosopher". See Allhoff & Monroe (2007), 13–30.

Tallis, R. 2003. *The Hand: A Philosophical Inquiry into Human Being*. Edinburgh: Edinburgh University Press.

Tallis, R. 2004. *I Am: A Philosophical Inquiry into First-Person Being*. Edinburgh: Edinburgh University Press.

Tallis, R. 2005. *The Knowing Animal: A Philosophical Inquiry into Knowledge and Truth*. Edinburgh: Edinburgh University Press.

Vernon, J. 2007. *Hunger: A Modern History*. Cambridge, MA: Harvard University Press.

Williams, C. K. 2007. "Danger". In *Signs and Humours: The Poetry of Medicine*, L. Greenlaw (ed.). London: Calouste Gulbenkian Foundation.

Index